Proverbial

Proverbial
stress busters

Great consolation may grow
out of the smallest saying

Lourens Schlebusch

HUMAN & ROUSSEAU
Cape Town Pretoria Johannesburg

Also by Lourens Schlebusch

Conduct Disorders in Youth
(Editor) **The Vulnerable: Understanding and Preventing Suicide**
Mind-Body Synthesis. The Interactive Health Care Equation
(Editor) **Suicidal Behaviour**
(Editor) **Clinical Health Psychology. A Behavioural Medicine Perspective**
(Editor) **A Basic Guide to the Diagnosis and Treatment of Depression**
(Editor) **Suicidal Behaviour 2**
(Editor) **Cancer Can Be Beaten: A Biopsychosocial Approach**
(Editor) **Suicidal Behaviour 3**
(Editor) **South Africa Beyond Transition: Psychological Wellbeing**

Videos/Audiotapes
Stress Management (Video)
Living With Cancer (Audiotape)
Maintenance of Self (Video)
Maintenance of Self (Audiotape)

Copyright © 1998 by Lourens Schlebusch
First published in 1998 by Human & Rousseau (Pty) Ltd
State House, 3-9 Rose Street, Cape Town
Cover design and typography by Annelize van Rooyen
Set in 12 on 14 pt Bembo by Human & Rousseau
Printed and bound by National Book Printers, Drukkery Street
Goodwood, Western Cape

ISBN 0 7981 3806 8

CONTENTS

Preface

Maxims are the condensed good sense of nations

A proverb is the wit of one and the wisdom of many

Stress has become the 'buzz' word of our times. Not all stress is bad for you, though. A certain amount is necessary to keep you functioning at your best. It is, therefore, important to distinguish between healthy and unhealthy stress. Unhealthy stress is likely to become *the disease* of the 21st century. It is believed to be associated with many psychological and physical ailments. Yet, most people find it hard to deal with. Why? Because they accept and live with it, because they don't really understand it, or simply because they don't know what to do about it? This doesn't have to be you. There is nothing mysterious about stress management. It is often simply a question of common sense. You'll be surprised at how easy it is for you to improve the quality of your life by doing something positive about your stress.

This book has been designed to assist you in doing just that. It has been written with the general reader in mind. After years of research and writing scientific manuscripts on the impact of stress on health and disease and leading stress-management workshops, I have come to realise the need for an easy-to-read guide on stress management based on some of the more important practical principles distilled from my work and that of others. Each principle is introduced with a maxim or proverb. I chose to do this because most human behaviour is covered by them in some way and because they are short and memorable statements of popular wisdom that contain analytical observations, warnings or advice. They are then placed in a modern psychological context of stress management along with other rele-

11

vant sayings. These will give you a basic understanding of stress and its symptoms and provide you with common-sense solutions which will go a long way towards helping you to cope with the stress in your life. *There is nothing new under the sun.* Ideas about the influence of stress on health and disease date from early writings of the Assyrians, Greeks and Romans. This book literally looks at old truths from a different perspective – that of current understanding and management of your stress. I have found such wider interpretation of proverbs valuable because of their metaphorical application to a broad range of human activities. I have taken the liberty in this book to use them to teach you about stress management.

Happy reading, and remember, *good words without deeds are rushes and reeds.* In line with current international thinking, a few words have been changed here and there to make the proverbs nonsexist; for example, I changed 'man', 'he', 'she' to 'person'; 'men', 'women', etc. to 'people'; 'himself' to 'the self'; etc. Where gender refers to 'wrath', 'animals', 'nature', etc. these words were changed to 'it'. A few of my own maxims are also included. They are: *Drive your car, don't let it drive you*; *Breathing bespeaks body and mind*; *The weakest link is the weakest think*; *Don't dig your grave with your teeth*; *If you whip up the wind, you must expect the waves*; *Those who have to wait on you always carry the smile*; and *Don't swop skills for pills.*

Several 'thank you's' are in order. Deanne Cavanagh has been invaluable in typing the manuscript. Isabel Cooke, my literary agent, provided the original idea for this book. Jo Orsmond created the cartoons. Jennifer Southgate worked closely with me during many of the stress-management workshops I presented. As Director of Lifestyle Promotion, an organisation that specialised in stress man-agement, assertiveness training, and cross-cultural communication, she was a continual source of inspiration and support during our many stimulating discussions.

Since some of the stress symptoms discussed in this book can also be associated with various medical conditions, I advise that you con-sult a medically qualified practioner to establish whether you require medical help. You may have a pre-existing medical problem that might require a medical consultation. Likewise, if you suffer from severe stress that you cannot cope with on your own you should consult an appropriate professional in the field.

Lourens Schlebusch
Durban, South Africa, 1998

Knowledge is power

What is stress?

This saying traditionally implies that the greater your knowledge, the greater your influence will be on others. But knowledge also helps you in other ways. In your daily life it can spell the difference between helplessness and mastering your stress. *A person that nothing questions, nothing learns*, and a Chinese proverb states that *learning is a treasure that accompanies its owner everywhere*. People may have good intentions and genuine earnestness in wanting to do something about their stress, but for many it's a case of *zeal without knowledge is a runaway horse*. Their enthusiasm without knowledge may not be helpful, and in some cases do more harm than good. So, appropriate

knowledge regarding stress management is important. A first step is to learn what is meant by the term **stress**, for *a mind enlightened is like heaven; a mind in darkness is like hell* (another Chinese proverb). Once you know what stress is, how it works and how it affects you, you can then turn your knowledge to mastering it. There are various competing definitions of stress, but for our purposes stress can be defined as your physiological, psychological and behavioural reactions when you attempt to adapt and adjust to internal and/or external demands and/or change. If you cannot cope with the stress within a reasonable period of time, it can become **unhealthy stress**. It can be associated with any action or situation that makes excessive physical or psychological demands on you that upset your equilibrium. A key issue is your adaptation, or failure to adapt, to such demands and/or changes in your life. If the stress is continuous and excessive or protracted and unrestrained and not adequately dealt with, your body's resources will be depleted eventually, and psychological and medical problems can result. In some instances it can be as critical as suggested in the saying: *Adapt or die.*

Seeing is believing

What is a stressor?

Traditionally, this proverb means that some people are reluctant to believe something unless they can see it. But for many, the way they see it can also make it a stressor. What is a stressor? Stress is caused by a stressor. A stressor can be any event, situation, person, illness, etc. that you perceive as stressful and induces your stress reaction. Stressors (or the causes of stress) can be innumerable and different people may respond differently to them. Although stressors are part of everyone's existence, some experience them more severely than others for various reasons, as you will see when you determine your position on the stress curve later on. Stress and change are inevitable. The inability to cope with change of any kind can be a major stressor. Although humankind has always been subjected to change, it is currently more prevalent than ever before and is occurring at an unprecedented rate. In fact,

the only real constant is that nothing is constant. This is captured in the saying that *there is nothing permanent except change,* taken from the theory of Heraclitus, the Greek philosopher, who maintained that the only reality is change. Even if you hang on to your old ways, you will find that you react to the changes around you. The reason for this is that while everything around you changes so rapidly all the time, in your modern lifestyle you are expected to meet and adjust constantly to the demands made on you by those changes. This, in turn, has a lot to do with your perception of the change. Accept that *times change and we with them.* This does not mean that you must reject what is good from the past, for sometimes *old shoes are easiest* and *old customs are best.* But if you adapt your views to change and keep up to date, you won't see and believe it to be stressful, and you'll be able to *preserve the old, but know the new,* as a Chinese proverb advises.

3 Necessity has no holiday

Stress and your nervous system

You survive because of your **nervous system**. It doesn't take a break when you do. Its purpose is to direct the complex processes of your body's internal environment and to serve as your body's link with the outside world. Without it, you wouldn't have the ability to see, hear, taste, smell, feel or receive incoming messages from the outside world, and would be unable to respond to heat, cold, food, water, danger, etc. There would be chaos within your body if each organ system acted independently. To understand your stress response, you need to understand how your **nervous system** is organised. Together with your **endocrine system** it acts continuously to maintain homeostasis (balance), enabling you to survive and to thrive. It is divided into two principal parts, your **central** and your **peripheral nervous systems**. Your **central nervous system** serves as the main control system of the body, and includes the brain and the spinal cord. Your **peripheral nervous system** is subdivided into the **somatic** and **autonomic** subdivisions. Many nerves and

receptors concerned with changes in your external environment are **somatic**, whereas many that regulate your internal environment are **autonomic**. The **autonomic nervous system** is autonomous, works automatically, and will even continue its activities when you are asleep.

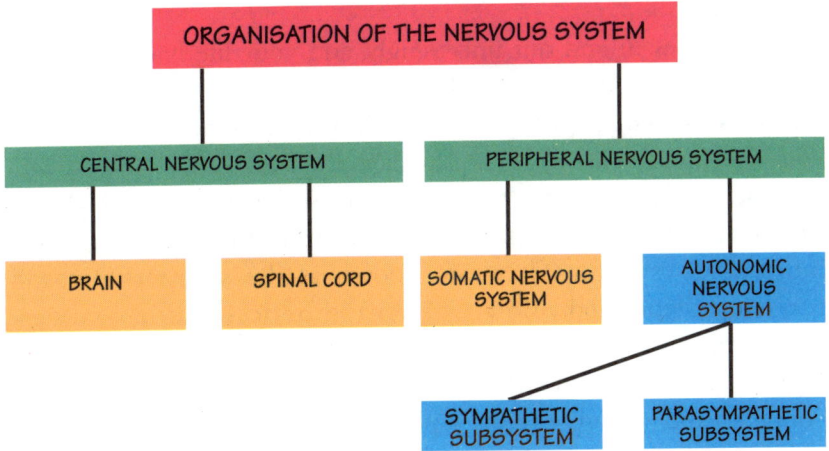

```
ORGANISATION OF THE NERVOUS SYSTEM
├── CENTRAL NERVOUS SYSTEM
│   ├── BRAIN
│   └── SPINAL CORD
└── PERIPHERAL NERVOUS SYSTEM
    ├── SOMATIC NERVOUS SYSTEM
    └── AUTONOMIC NERVOUS SYSTEM
        ├── SYMPATHETIC SUBSYSTEM
        └── PARASYMPATHETIC SUBSYSTEM
```

4 Every flow must have its ebb

Your autonomic nervous system

The tide goes in and out unceasingly, and your life has similar ups and downs. Your body responds to stress likewise. Your **autonomic nervous system** largely participates in the involuntary activities of your body and controls amongst others the heart, glands, blood vessels and internal organs. It regulates major vegetative (bodily) and stress-dependent functions of your body. It, in turn, can be divided into two subsystems. These are known as the **sympathetic** and parasympathetic subdivisions. The **sympathetic subdivision** operates to stimulate organs and to mobilise energy, especially in response to stress. In contrast, the **parasympathetic subdivision** operates to conserve and restore energy, especially when you are engaged in quiet or calm activities. Many of your body's organs are stimulated by both subdivisions which act in an antagonistic way. For example, your heart rate is quickened by messages from your **sympathetic nerves** in response to stress, and slowed by messages from your **parasympathetic nerves** after you've dealt with the stress. Let's look at these activities more closely in terms of the stress response.

The Autonomic Nervous System

Sympathetic and Parasympathetic Nervous System

These two parts of the autonomic nervous system affect many of the same bodily organs, but in opposite ways.

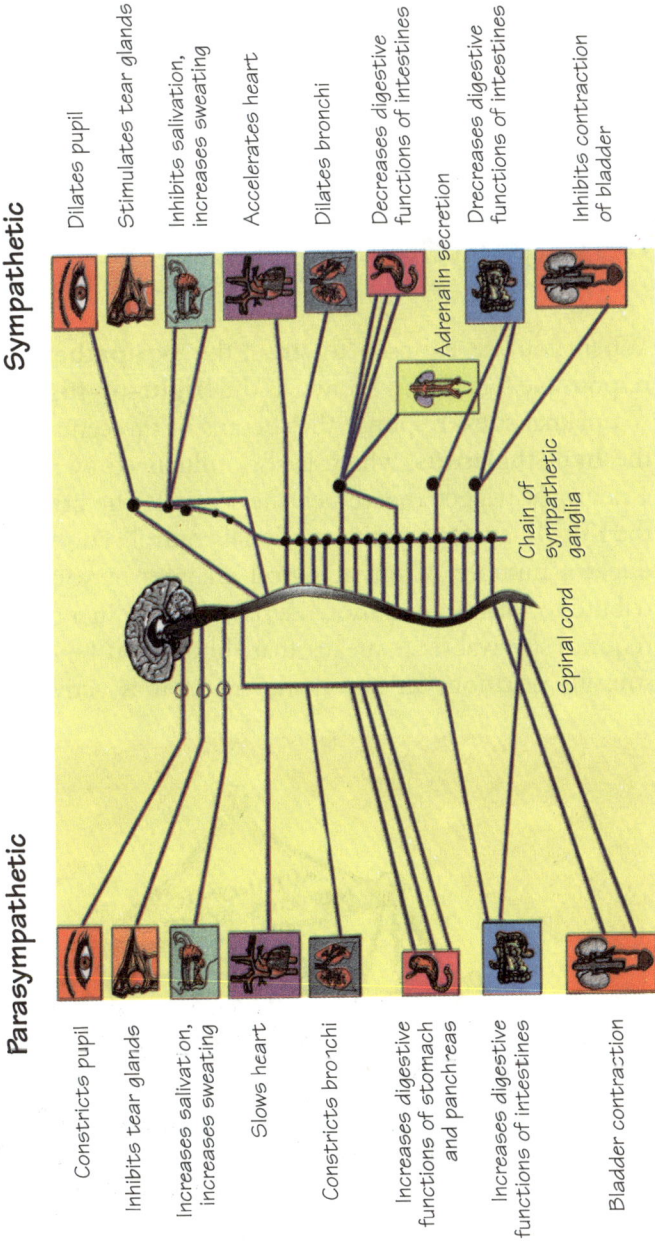

Sympathetic

- Dilates pupil
- Stimulates tear glands
- Inhibits salivation, increases sweating
- Accelerates heart
- Dilates bronchi
- Decreases digestive functions of intestines
- Adrenalin secretion
- Drecreases digestive functions of intestines
- Inhibits contraction of bladder

Chain of sympathetic ganglia

Spinal cord

Parasympathetic

- Constricts pupil
- Inhibits tear glands
- Increases salivation, increases sweating
- Slows heart
- Constricts bronchi
- Increases digestive functions of stomach and pancreas
- Increases digestive functions of intestines
- Bladder contraction

5 Safety lies in the middle course

The subsystems of your autonomic nervous system

When you are exposed to stress, the **sympathetic subsystem** is responsible for what is known as the **'fight-or-flight'** response. This is a primal stress response that begins in the centre of your brain in the **hypothalamus,** which is also influenced by the **amygdala** via a neuronal trigger (nerve cell messenger). The **amygdala** is part of the **limbic system,** your emotional control centre. This process produces a number of physiological changes in your body that contribute to making you more alert and active in a crisis situation that requires survival. This means that should you be confronted with a stressful situation, an automatic reaction is activated within your

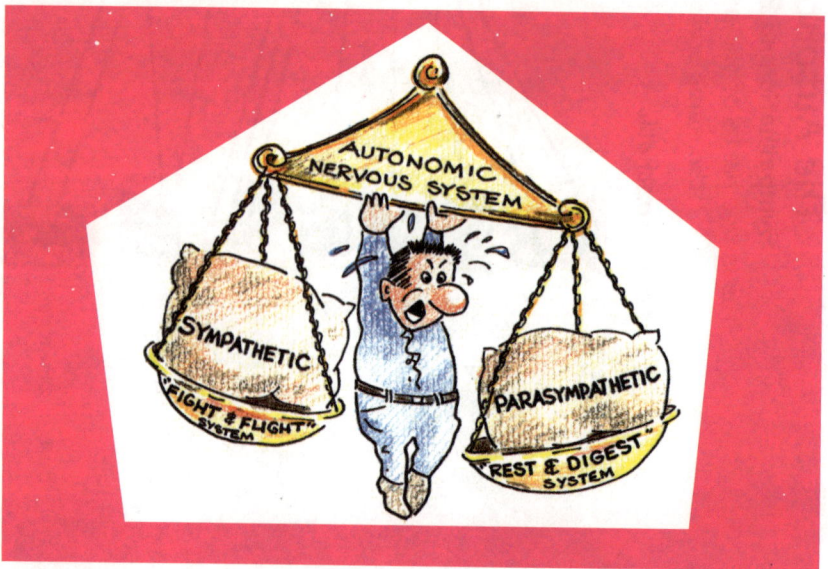

body. There is an increase in heart rate, respiration (breathing), and so on to enable you to deal immediately with the situation. This subsystem can be compared to the accelerator of your car.

The second part of the subdivision is known as the **parasympathetic subsystem**. It serves as a balance which, after a stress response, will tend to slow things down to return to normal. It is sometimes referred to as the **'rest-and-recovery'** or **'rest-and-digest'** phase. This subsystem can be compared to the brake of your car.

Both systems are involved when you attempt to deal with stress. The one acts as an accelerator and the other as a brake. What you need to aim for is a balance. *Drive your car, don't let it drive you.* You don't want to accelerate out of control, but you also don't want to brake so hard that your life comes to a standstill, for *measure is a merry mean.*

It takes two to tango

Your nervous and endocrine systems

This saying emphasises joint responsibility. Likewise, the **nervous** and **endocrine systems** jointly regulate life processes. They continuously monitor your body's activities, and adjust them appropriately, so that they are maintained in a steady state. They are both involved in your stress response. In their case it's a case of *that which two will, takes effect*.

Stress causes chemical and other changes which affect the physical, psychological and hormonal balance of your body. In particular, the endocrine system is involved in this. It consists of a series of glands without ducts, known as the **endocrine glands**, that secrete hormones (chemical messengers) to help regulate the activities of other tissues and organs. The principal **endocrine glands** are illustrated here.

Stress and the endocrine system

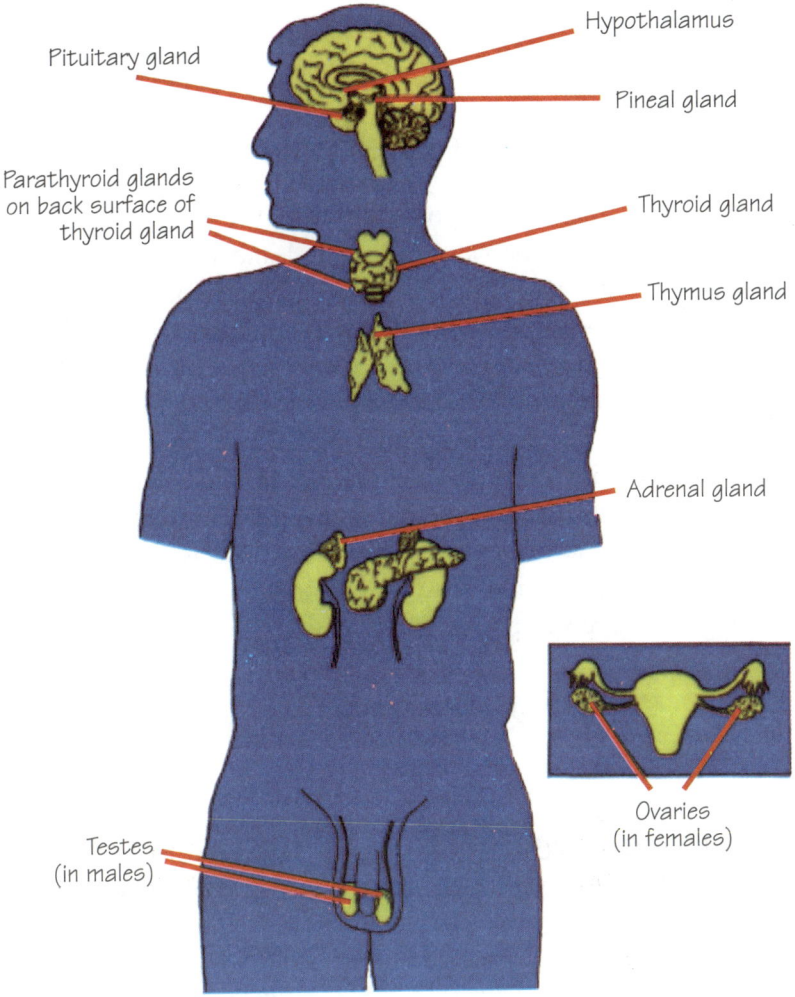

Hypothalamus

Pituitary gland

Pineal gland

Parathyroid glands
on back surface of
thyroid gland

Thyroid gland

Thymus gland

Adrenal gland

Ovaries
(in females)

Testes
(in males)

7 There are more ways to the wood than one

The two pathways of stress

Inasmuch as there are different means to arrive at the same objective, there are different routes to exploring your stress response. As you have seen, the stress response is a complex process that involves the interrelationship between your mind and body. It is useful to conceptualise the way you process stress via two basic pathways. These include a **physiological pathway** and a **psychological pathway**. The **physiological pathway** is subconscious in that it contains physical and emotional responses that act to prepare your body for action. The **psychological pathway** is conscious and voluntary in that it involves responses that occur when you perceive and evaluate the stressors. Although they involve different routes, they arrive at a common objective, because in this case *all roads lead to Rome*. Both keep you in a state of readiness and operate together to produce your stress response.

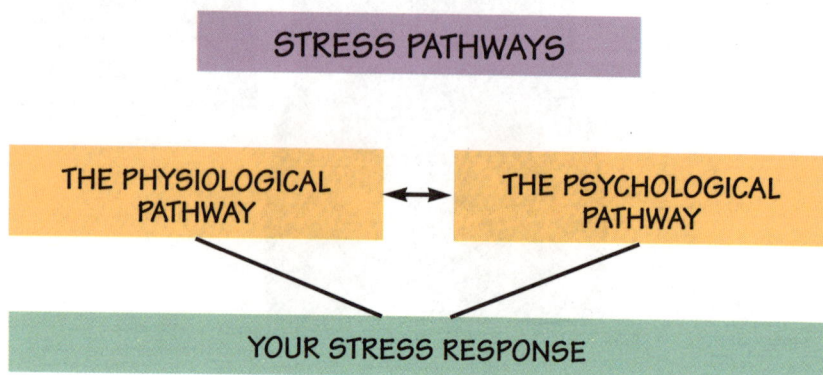

STRESS PATHWAYS

| THE PHYSIOLOGICAL PATHWAY | ←→ | THE PSYCHOLOGICAL PATHWAY |

YOUR STRESS RESPONSE

8 Forewarned is forearmed

The physiological pathway

Modern research on the stress response has developed rapidly, but as early as 1831, during the Industrial Revolution, James Johnson (a London physician) spoke about what he called the wear-and-tear complaint. About a century later (in the 1920s), Walter Cannon at Harvard University proved the basic primal stress response which follows a sequence that is seemingly a consequence of eons of evolution. This he called the **'fight-or-flight'** response, a concept refined by subsequent research. The **physiological pathway** involves the **autonomic nervous system** and the **endocrine system**, which results in your stress response. When you are confronted with a stressor, there is an automatic physiological reaction in your body that prepares you for the 'fight-or-flight' response. In brief, the biochemistry and physiology of the stress response takes place stepwise, almost like a cascade where the previous step or phase affects the next one. In the case of too much stress, if you are warned beforehand that something stressful is going to happen, you are able to take the necessary steps in advance. In the same way *force without forecast is of little avail*, which implies that if you foresee problems and are prepared for them, this would be of more use to you than great strength or skill. The same principle is embodied in the proverb *forecast is better than work-hard*. For example, prior knowledge about a pending operation or treatment for disease can minimise the expected stress, especially if you are overreacting and imagining the worst. Likewise, you can take appropriate precautions in expected crises such as when there are flood predictions or when you anticipate losing a loved one.

THE STRESS CASCADE

STRESSOR

STRESS
(INFLUENCED BY YOUR PERCEPTION)

ACTIVATION OF THE AMYGDALA IN THE MID-BRAIN
(PART OF THE LIMBIC SYSTEM, YOUR EMOTIONAL CONTROL CENTRE)

NEURONAL RESPONSE
(NERVE CELL MESSENGERS)

AUTONOMIC NERVOUS SYSTEM

TRIGGERS THE HYPOTHALAMUS

HORMONAL RESPONSE
(CHEMICAL MESSENGERS)

RELEASE OF THE CORTICOTROPIN-RELEASING FACTOR
(CRF HORMONAL RESPONSE)

TRIGGERS THE PITUITARY

HORMONAL RESPONSE

RELEASES THE ADRENOCORTICOTROPIC HORMONE
(ACTH HORMONAL RESPONSE)

STIMULATION OF ADRENAL GLANDS

ADRENAL MEDULLA	ADRENAL CORTEX
HORMONAL SECRETION	HORMONAL SECRETION
RELEASE OF HORMONES *EPINEPHRINE (ADRENALINE)* *NOREPINEPHRINE (NORADRENALINE)*	RELEASE OF HORMONES *CORTISOL* *ALDOSTERONE*
INCREASES YOUR HEART RATE, METABOLIC RATE, AND STRENGTH OF MUSCLE CONTRACTIONS, AND REROUTES YOUR BLOOD TO ORGANS THAT NEED MORE IN TIMES OF STRESS	MOBILISES FAT, CONVERTS OTHER NUTRIENTS TO GLUCOSE, AND RAISES YOUR BLOOD SUGAR LEVEL

YOUR STRESS RESPONSE

9 Stress is in the eye of the beholder

The psychological pathway

The **psychological pathway** involves the way you see stress. Stress does not exist by itself, nor is it only a physiological response. It exists in your consciousness as well. This depends on your perception of the stress in your life, and your assessment of whether the stress is harmful to you or whether it is necessary so that you can function optimally. Perception is a psychological function that helps you to organise and interpret stimuli from your environment. In other words, based on how you look at the stressor, the **psychological pathway** helps you with coping skills and to decide whether the stress is positive and to your advantage, or negative and to your disadvantage. The thinking part of your brain, your appraisal of the stress, and your decision-making abilities and coping skills are all important factors in this process. Since the way you look at the stress and your ability to deal with it play important roles in how you are affected by it, your perceptions can produce thoughts which in turn can produce emotions and feelings which in turn can result in related stress behaviour. It is a question of *beware of no person more than thyself*, and literally a case of *what the eye doesn't see the heart doesn't grieve over*. You will not be worried or distressed by the stressor if you are unaware that it is a stressor. So *don't cry before you are hurt* and *don't meet troubles halfway*, for *our worst misfortunes are those that never befall us*.

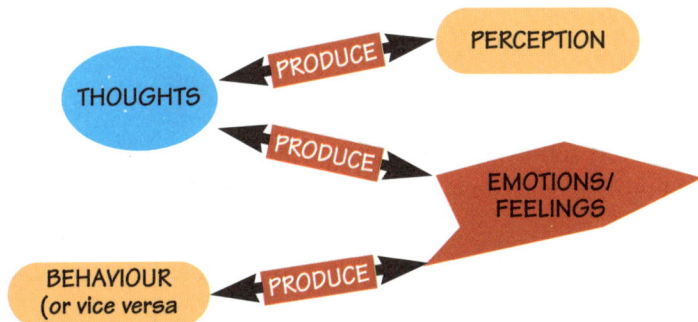

29

10 No gain without pain

Some stress is healthy

You are unlikely to achieve much without some trouble or hardship. Likewise, not all stress is bad for you. The proverb *nothing seek, nothing find* teaches initiative and the fact that you cannot achieve success without effort. It might not always be easy for you to achieve success, but *nothing succeeds like success*. Once you've harnessed healthy stress to achieve success, you'll be on your way to even more prosperity. Some measure of healthy stress is a necessity of diligence. Healthy stress spurs you on to achieve better by providing the energy and motivation for you to do your best. This positive stress is called **eustress**, which should be your aim. Healthy stress includes:

◆ delivering a high standard of work
◆ a good information flow and meeting deadlines
◆ confident decision making and effective problem-solving skills
◆ co-operative behaviour and encouraging harmonious relationships
◆ good concentration, attendance and time-keeping
◆ a positive and cheerful manner and an appropriate sense of humour
◆ expressing concern and care for others

It leads to:
◆ clear thinking and good long-term planning
◆ plenty of energy and a high level of motivation
◆ setting realistic expectations for yourself
◆ enhanced achievements, being positive and constructive
◆ feeling that you are a valued and successful member of society

11 Of idleness comes no goodness

Understress is unhealthy

Although you are focusing on overstress right now, don't forget that understress can be equally bad. In other words, an idle, unstimulating, lethargic lifestyle can also be unhealthy. *Idleness turns the edge of wit* and *a lazy sheep thinks its wool heavy*.

In addition, the absence of stress itself can be stressful. Physical and psychological isolation taken to extremes can be disastrous. Inasmuch as you cannot tolerate stress overload, you cannot tolerate severe underload. When your stress levels drop too low for normal stimulation, you are in trouble. To counteract that you should seek to balance your lifestyle so that you maintain a steady, satisfying level of stress and avoid understress, for not only is it true that *you can have too much of a good thing*, but *standing pools gather filth*.

12 Extremes are dangerous

Overstress is unhealthy

This proverb implies that anything (virtues, beliefs, emotions, activity, etc.) indulged in too excessively could approach the opposite extreme. Exactly the same happens with stress where often *every extremity is a fault.* Quite often when you are confronted by stress, it's not possible for you to either fight it or run away from it. It would hardly be considered good practice for you to club your boss over the head and drag him off to some cave, or to run away like a coward. You have to stay and face it. This means that your traditional 'fight-or-flight' response won't help you out. As a result, if you have not learnt different coping skills, and you cannot effectively deal with the stress, you remain in an aroused or activated state of stress for a protracted length of time. Your **parasympathetic**, or **'rest-and-digest'** phase doesn't get sufficient chance to slow your body down, so your stress is taken to extremes. Consequently, there can be a damaging effect on your psychological and physical wellbeing. Likewise, too little stress can be taken to extremes and cause you harm.

So, to summarise, your reaction to stress is natural and normal. It occurs automatically and serves to activate you to perform optimally. If, however, it is prolonged and intense, and you cannot cope with it effectively, or when you live an unstimulating, lethargic lifestyle with persistent understress, it results in the disruption of your normal life and routine. It then produces **dis**tress or **dis**ease. This does not necessarily have to be your fate, because you can acquire alternative coping skills and learn that while *a little wind kindles, much puts out the fire.*

13

A bow long bent at last waxes weak

The General Adaptation Syndrome

There are limitations to your body's endurance and ability to cope with stress. Hans Selye (an eminent pioneer from Montreal, working in stress research) who wrote the first book exclusively devoted to stress in 1950, coined the term **eustress** (positive stress) and devised the concept of the **General Adaptation Syndrome** (GAS) which has three phases that illustrate the basic stress response. Stage one of the GAS is called the **alarm phase**. In this phase you are in a general state of arousal or activation, but with no specific organ being negatively affected yet. This allows you to fight or flee (the fight-or-flight response). In stage two, your body becomes used to stress if it is continued for a long enough period that cannot be avoided. This is called the **adaptation phase** or phase of resistance. During this

phase your body's physiological responses are above normal, which also then makes you more susceptible to other stressors. In the third stage, the **phase of exhaustion**, the organ systems or processes in your body which are dealing with the stress break down and you become vulnerable to more serious psychological and physical problems. The very reactions that allowed your body in the first place to deal with short-term stressors during the first stage (for example, increased energy, tensing of muscles in readiness for action, increase in blood pressure, etc.) can in this last stage become unhealthy as long-term responses. For example, your tense muscles can result in pain, and other stress-related disorders can ultimately develop, because eventually *the orange that is too hard squeezed yields a bitter juice*, and *too long burden makes weary bones*.

14 The spirit is willing, but the flesh is weak

Stress and your physical health

The mind-body connection is not new. Many ancient scholars and philosophers have commented on it. Plato stated in the fourth century BC that *all diseases of the body proceed from the mind or soul.* Various medical conditions have been shown to be associated with stress, both directly and indirectly. They can either cause stress, or be caused by stress. Stress affects a whole range of bodily functions, including your: perceptual senses, nervous system, hormonal balance, cardio-

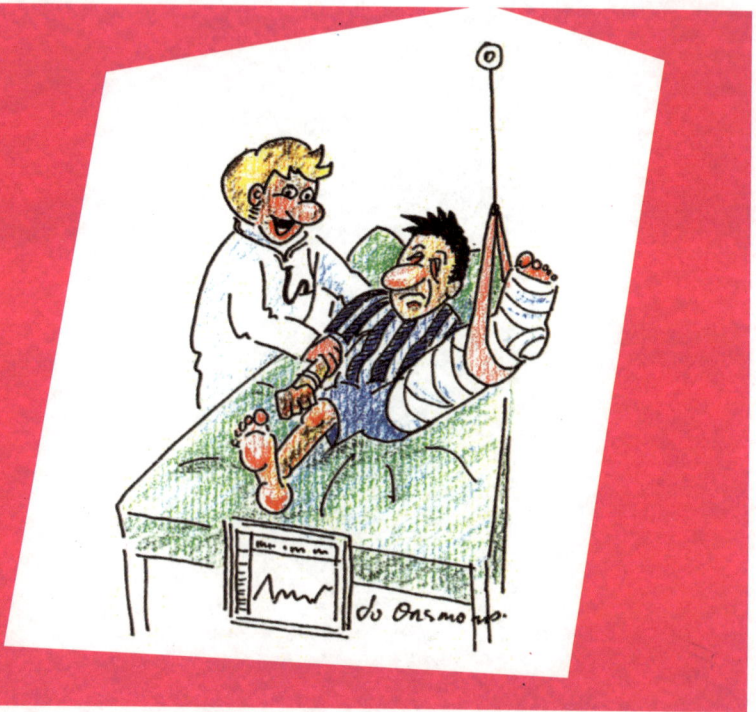

vascular system, digestive system, respiratory function, skin, urogenital system, and your immune system. Extreme stress can even result in death. In certain traditional societies extreme stress is sometimes deliberately applied as punishment within a specific cultural context, as seen in, for example, the practice of voodoo or the recital of fateful incantations and rituals that can place the victim under the spell of death. Stress can especially suppress your **immune system** and lead to poor immuno-competence. When the **immune system** is compromised by stress, your body's natural resistance to fight off disease is impaired. Your body's immune response depends upon its ability to distinguish between your body itself and foreign matter. So, in a way your **immune system** acts as your body's own surveillance mechanism which serves to protect it from attacks on normal body tissue, and helps to resist or fight disease. Your mind and body function holistically and not as separate entities. Your social and spiritual life are important in this process. So change your perception to a more person-focused rather than a disease-focused one. Health is not just the absence of disease but a state of complete physical, psychological and social wellbeing. It is not only true that *health is better than wealth*, but also that *health is great riches*.

15 Too much spoils, too little does not satisfy

Your rating on the stress curve

The implications in this maxim are that without the drive that stress provides you will achieve little, but that you must not pass the peak of your stress curve. The stress that you encounter affects your position on the stress curve. Your position on this curve is dynamic and varies according to many factors. These include: your stress thresholds, age and phase of life, the time of day, coping skills, personality characteristics, level of fitness, health, diet, lifestyle, and the nature and meaning of stress for you which are influenced by your perception of the stress. Take a look at the stress curve and see where you fit. Do this regularly and aim for optimum stress, for *measure is treasure*. If you do not recognise the signs of negative stress that interfere with your optimum performance, you are at risk of progressively moving into the negative parts of the stress curve. Your aim should not be to achieve the undesirable or even impossible goal to eliminate all stress from your life, but to achieve just the right amount of stress so that you stay in the positive phase of the stress curve.

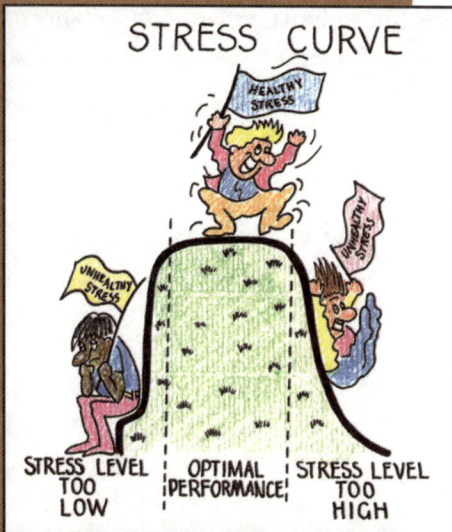

16 A leopard cannot change its spots

Stress and your skin

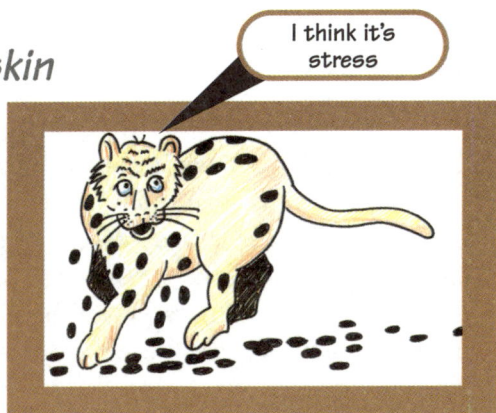

I think it's stress

This proverb means that it is hard to change your character, or that there is no more chance of changing than there is of a leopard changing its spots. However, in terms of the stress response, your skin is also often one of the first to show the effects of long-term stress because of its obvious visibility. A stress-ravaged skin has been referred to as the 'careworn countenance' of premature old age. Our leopard was not only unable to change its spots, but because of his stress has now lost them. Since your skin is a common target organ for unhealthy stress, it can respond to a variety of external and internal factors, including your diet, and reflects your health or ill-health and other responses in different ways. This is nicely illustrated in the sayings *sickness shows us what we are* and *health and gaiety foster beauty*. Obvious reactions include: turning pale with fear, blushing with embarrassment, reddening with rage, etc. Other stress-related changes occur; for example, during the fight-or-flight response blood drains from the vessels near the skin and its clotting time shortens so that you will lose less blood in case your body is wounded, and the skin perspires to get rid of waste and to cool your body through evaporation. In addition, stress is associated with several dermatological conditions, such as **contact dermatitis**, **urticaria** (which has been referred to as 'suppressed weeping'), **neurodermatitis**, **eczema**, **psoriasis**, **alopaecia areata** (patchy hair loss), etc. The cause of 80% of skin problems is psychological.

The mind is the person

Stress and your psychological health

Stress can be associated with many psychological problems. Your perception and thinking are important in this process. In the words of Descartes, *I think, therefore, I am* (*cogito, ergo sum*), and *it is the riches of the mind only that make a person rich and happy.* You have a highly developed brain and because you have the ability to think, you also have the ability to worry, even about symbolic or imagined threats. The anticipation of an event can sometimes be more stressful than the event itself. Don't add to your difficulties by worrying about what might happen in the future. All you'll do is create anticipatory anxiety and more stress. So *let your trouble tarry till its own day comes.* As with stress–related medical problems, some people are more susceptible to developing psychological problems because of stress, whereas in others it makes existing ones worse.

Psychological problems more specifically associated with stress can include:

suicidal behaviour

adjustment disorders

anxiety disorders — including acute stress disorder and posttraumatic stress disorder

depressive disorders

factitious disorders — an intentional production and misrepresentation of psychological or physical symptoms in order to assume a sick role or to be a patient

somatoform disorders — certain disorders related to somatisation where you translate stress into physical symptoms such as pain, nausea, etc. for which there are no appropriate medical explanations

pain and violence

substance-related disorders

sexual disorders

burnout

dissociative disorders — a sudden, temporary alteration in normally integrated functions of consciousness, identity or motor behaviour

sleep disorders — sleep disturbances and persistent fatigue are in themselves frequently symptomatic of other stress-related psychological problems such as depression

18 Life would be too smooth if it had no rubs in it

Stress and life events

You can't expect a stress-free life. Both life events and daily hassles can be associated with stress in a cause-and-effect way. **Life events** include major events such as the death of a loved one, a major personal injury, exposure to a traumatic event, marriage, separation, crises, etc. These can also sometimes be the basis for chronic stress. **Daily hassles** refer to the daily grind that produces irritations and frustrations in your everyday routine life derived from modern living, such as crowds, losing keys, financial pressures, tending to sick animals, traffic jams, noise, pollution, work pressures, relationships, arguments, **technostress**, etc. Technology is supposed to work for you, but sometimes it is a significant cause of stress, called **technostress**. Just think, for example, how you react when things grind to a halt because of a computer glitch or the ATM is faulty when you need money quickly. These events are often the basis for acute stress, because of the daily worry they cause you. Not only does anticipatory anxiety cause stress, so does the lack of it. An unanticipated event (pleasant or unpleasant) or unexpected bad news can have significant effects on stress. Take the example of the near-miss accident when driving a car. You react instantly without much time to think. But once the shakiness is gone, hours (even days) later fantasies of 'what if' this or that had happened can recur in your waking hours or dreams, causing you stress. To deal effectively with stress, it is important to identify the sources of stress in your life (both long-term and daily hassles), as well as how your lifestyle contributes to them, and then make the necessary adaptive changes.

IDENTIFY THE SOURCES OF STRESS IN YOUR LIFE		
Work environment		✗
Relationships	✔	
Technostress	✔	

19 Envy eats nothing but its own heart

Be comfortable with the success of others

A Hindi proverb teaches that *true happiness consists in making happy*. So be happy for others if they achieve. Don't let their success cause you stress because of envy and your own unresolved needs. *Envy shoots at others, and wounds the self* and *a person who admits envy admits inferiority*. You may feel inferior because of a faulty perception that you are inadequate or incompetent. Often this is due to self-expectations that are beyond your range of challenge or that are unrealistic. Don't compare yourself with others in order to lose, because this will maintain your negative self-image. *It is comparison that makes people happy or miserable*. Your happiness or success is success in your own right, and although *you can't win them all*, an Arabic proverb teaches that *a person learns little from success, but much from failure*. Accept that in life *you win some, you lose some* and only *the vulgar will keep no account of your hits, but of your misses*.

20 A contented mind is a perpetual feast

Practise relaxation

Don't forget that contentment causes lasting happiness. *Content is happiness.* Both positive and negative stress is omnipresent in your life. You cannot avoid it. Any physical or psychological effort requires it to various degrees. For some, stress has been a turning point in their lives while for others it has caused serious problems. Some react to it with mysterious passion, while others pine away from maladies without obvious physical cause. For some (the so-called stress-seekers) it can become as addictive as a drug. They have to function on the edge to get excitement. Stress results in psychological, behavioural and physiological reactions. This produces that keyed-up feeling which can mobilise the sports contestant to achieve the ultimate or push others beyond their levels of tolerance. Mental and physical relaxation are excellent ways to cope with that keyed-up feeling. This includes specific relaxation techniques (of which there are many available), meditation and practising activities like yoga. Westerners' quest for stress relief has often led them to the East. But some activities such as meditation do not necessarily require deep familiarity with Eastern religions. Although some require more skill and effort, a simple quiet time of ten to twenty minutes twice daily where you focus on correct breathing and a quiet, peaceful mindset can be very effective. Practices like meditation and yoga will not only help you with stress, but can lower blood pressure, improve your brain function, and help with various physical and psychological problems. But you should also strive for contentment, for *content is the philosopher's stone, that turns all it touches into gold.* So get enough rest and feed your body, mind and soul.

21 Bacchus has drowned more people than Neptune

Alcohol abuse

Bacchus is the Roman god of wine, and Neptune is the Roman god of the sea. Alcohol, tobacco, and the abuse of other substances are common but harmful responses to stress. Smoking is associated with cancer and many other diseases. Even one cigarette can make your heart work harder within a minute and cause temporary loss of flexibility and elasticity in your **aorta** (a main artery) for as long as twenty minutes. Throbbing headaches resulting from overenthusiastic consumption of alcohol (due to its breakdown products, especially constituents called congeners), and the negative effects on productivity are legion. Alcohol abuse depletes the body of blood sugar, creating weakness, nervousness, perspiring and tremors. It causes sleep disturbances; depresses dream sleep; produces a surge of metabolic activity in the speech area of the brain resulting in talkativeness and slurring; depresses regions of the brain that co-ordinate movement, making the person stagger; and affects the **limbic system** (the emotional centre of the brain) resulting in problems with sexual activity, violence, boisterousness, etc. In terms of stress management and alcohol abuse, there is no better advice than *Adam's ale is the best brew* (Adam's ale is an old term for good old-fashioned water). According to a Chinese proverb, *drunkenness does not produce faults, it discovers them*. Apart from treating the diseases that substance abuse cause, just think of the staggering health and financial costs that come in the wake of accidents and violence associated with alcohol abuse, and accidental fires and burns caused by careless smokers. Substance abuse not only causes stress, but the subsequent consequences on your health can contribute directly to a progressively decreasing ability to combat stress.

A stitch in time saves nine

Accident proneness

Prompt action at an early stage may prevent serious trouble later. Likewise there is a reciprocal relationship between stress and accident proneness. So, an effective way to prevent accidents and to reduce accident proneness is to reduce your stress levels early. Have you ever noticed how poor concentration and some of the other symptoms of stress can make you clumsy? Because of the fight-or-flight response and the resultant changes in you, especially muscle tension which prepares you for physical action, you are more likely to have accidents under high levels of stress. Stress, therefore, affects your health directly and indirectly, such as when it leads to accidents – especially when you overreact to stress-inducing situations. Your perception of the stress and your resultant stress response can make the situation worse and make you even more accident-prone. This applies across the spectrum of your life, but especially in traffic and work situations. The simultaneous intake of medication and other substances can make the situation even worse. Of course, accidents can in their own right either cause stress or increase it. It is better for you to deal with your stress timeously and to take precautions against stress-related accidents than to have to cope with the damage after they have occurred. *Prevention is better than cure.*

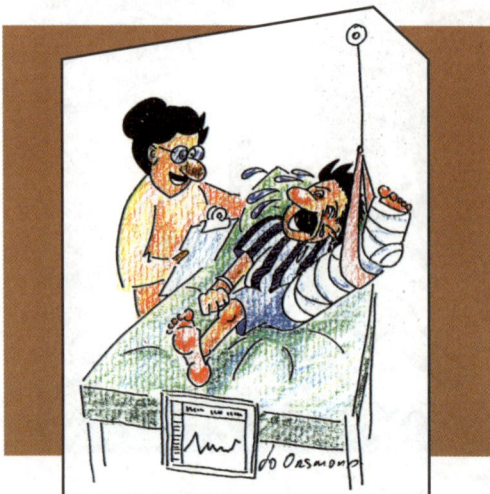

23 Travel makes a wise person better, but a fool worse

Stress and commuting

Many people take their stress out on the roads, and some are at their self-destructive worst when they get behind the wheel of a motor vehicle. Commuting itself is known to be a major stressor. Traffic congestion, road repairs, road hogs, pollution, noise, speed, etc. can all contribute to this. In addition, reckless or irresponsible driving is a distinct health-risk behaviour, because of the risk of accidents. This is made worse when you drive under the influence of certain substances, such as alcohol, or when you take certain medications that affect your concentration and responses. Not only are drivers at risk, but the occupants of vehicles as well as pedestrians can be seriously hurt, and the spiralling effects of such accidents cause significant stress to surviving relatives and friends, and usually have significant financial implications as a result. There is a saying about running your business effectively that states: *Drive your business, do not let it drive you.*

In terms of stress and driving it would be prudent to substitute 'business' for 'car': *Drive your car, do not let it drive you.*

24 Make not the stomach an apothecary's shop

The abuse of medicine

Substance abuse does not only include the abuse of alcohol, cigarettes and other drugs but also medicines. Don't rely too heavily on medicines to relieve stress. They might sometimes have a place, but abuse of medicine to deal with stress can make the stress worse, or ultimately result in medical or psychological problems. Like so many antistress programmes and methods for stress management, medicines support a vast, flourishing stress industry. This obviously leads to abuse. Inasmuch as some popular 'stress relievers' are loaded with potential danger for the consumer, so is the abuse of medicine. Such abuse commonly starts with taking certain medicines for stress-related problems without appropriate health-care supervision, which sets off a vicious cycle, even leading to substance-seeking behaviour, doctor shopping or pharmacy hopping. Don't forget that *measure is medicine*. Painkillers are one of the commonest medicinal substances which are abused. Stress is often associated with muscular pain and tension headaches for which painkillers are taken and eventually abused. Such abuse is also a major problem in suicidal behaviour involving self-poisoning, which accounts for a significant number of suicidal overdose patients being admitted to clinics and hospitals. So, *don't swop skills for pills*.

25 To be or not to be: that is the question

Stress and suicidal behaviour

In this well-known quotation, Hamlet meditates on suicide and the afterlife.

> To be, or not to be: that is the question:
> Whether 'tis nobler in the mind to suffer
> The slings and arrows of outrageous fortune,
> Or to take arms against a sea of troubles,
> And by opposing end them? To die: to sleep;
> No more; and, by a sleep to say we end
> The heart-ache and the thousand natural shocks
> That flesh is heir to, 'tis a consummation
> Devoutly to be wish'd.
>
> (Shakespeare, *Hamlet*, Act III, Scene I)

Stress is a major risk factor for suicidal behaviour. Suicidal behaviour is not an act of cowardice and has many faces. For example, it sometimes looks like an accident, or it can result from playing Russian roulette with your life where the decision to live or die is left to fate. Suicidal behaviour is an expression of behaviour and not a psychological disorder. It is a symptom of a psychological problem, and although it can be associated with stress, it can also be associated with other factors such as, for example, depression or another psychological disorder, or hopelessness. Apart from other factors and the need to treat the underlying disorder if present, suicidal behaviour can be construed from the perspective of two constructs: the person's levels of lethality (the seriousness of the method) and of distress. It is prudent not to simply remove the method, but also to address the level of distress urgently. If the distress levels can be brought down, the suicidal person frequently would automatically reduce the level of lethality (for example, come down from the ledge, hand over the gun, drive more carefully, put down the pills intended for the overdose, etc.).

26 If it were not for hope, the heart would break

Don't give up hope

When things are stressful, what prevents you from giving up or despairing is the hope that things will get better. In particular, a feeling of hopelessness, coupled with other symptoms of stress or depression, could result in suicidal thoughts and behaviour. Hopelessness tends to develop because of continuous negative expectations of the future. This is largely affected by your perception and resultant thoughts that your future holds little promise of the issues that cause you psychological pain and stress being resolved. *Hope is grief's best music*, and *hope keeps people alive*. Although the outlook for you may be grim, don't give up hope. *While there is life, there is hope*. It is in your nature as a human being to look forward to better times, despite setbacks. Don't deny yourself that, for *hope springs eternal in the human breast*.

Feelings of worthlessness

+

Depression

+

Hopelessness

=

Possible suicidal ideation

27 If in *excess even nectar* is poison

Overload

Stress is often associated with overload. When this happens you are at risk of reverting to more primitive behaviour and means of coping, and reactions such as denial of reality, avoidance behaviour and playing ostrich by pretending the problems don't exist or will go away. You are literally overstimulated and the demands made on you completely exceed your capacity to meet them. Information and demands pile up faster than your ability to process them, there are no solutions in sight and you are unable to improvise. Critical causes of overload are taking on too much, excessive time pressures, excessive responsibility, excessive expectations, and poor support systems. Don't overload yourself because of excessive expected monetary rewards and the need to have more and more when you already have sufficient. The saying *money is the root of all evil* is in fact a misquotation. More correctly *the love of money is the root of all evil*, which could lead to more stress. This implies that all sorts of tribulations can result from the desire to be rich.

Overload can be prevented by good self-management, and by not committing yourself to too many things at the same time. Therefore, *take no more on than you're able to bear*. Don't be too ambitious and be aware of your own limitations. Seek appropriate support, but remember, *books and friends should be few but good*. That is, it is better that they should be fewer and of good quality than many and drain you even more.

28 Don't have too many irons in the fire

Burnout

Persistent overload can lead to burnout. In the past, when horses were the main form of transport, blacksmiths were in great demand. They had 'irons in the fire' which they used for forging into horseshoes. If a blacksmith was very busy, he might have tried to save time by placing too many irons in his furnace, thereby creating a situation where there was insufficient heat to make them red hot. The proper meaning of the above proverb is that if you try and do too much at once, you won't do anything properly. However, in terms of stress management, if you have 'too many irons in the fire' and too much on the go at the same time, you run the risk of developing burnout and then you will not finish everything properly, as is also illustrated by the saying: *A person who begins many things finishes but few.* When the demands you are faced with are so excessive that a prolonged

and inordinate stress response is aroused, you pass your optimum level of functioning and enter a negative phase of stress which leads to mental and physical fatigue. This in turn can result in total mental or physical exhaustion – or 'burnout' – because *too much ought is good for nought*. This usually happens in the **phase of exhaustion** of the General Adaptation Syndrome discussed before. Avoid burnout by understanding the condition and its causes, by adopting more realistic ambitions, by improving your working and living conditions and seeking satisfaction in these areas, and by dealing with the stress associated with it.

Pleasant hours fly past

A positive psychological climate

When you enjoy yourself, time passes quickly. But it passes slowly when you are bored, have nothing to do, or work or play in an uncongenial environment. A positive psychological climate in the workplace and at home is necessary to keep stress to a minimum. A

family's or a company's stress levels are easily reflected in the stress levels of its members or employees. Just as you can find yourself in the positive or negative phase of the stress curve with its positive or negative consequences, so can the company that you work for. Incidentally, favourable working conditions (good pay, equipment, working hours, fringe benefits, procedures, etc.) and a healthy physical working environment will reduce worker dissatisfaction, resentment and ultimately stress. Poor physical working conditions, low productivity and stress are often associated with the 'sick building syndrome' and the symptoms it produces in workers: irritations of eyes, nose and throat; neurasthenic symptoms (headaches, dizziness, fatigue, confusion, nausea); skin irritation; hypersensitivity reactions (for example, nonasthmatics manifest asthma-like symptoms); and unpleasant odour and taste sensations. Each section of a company forms a part of the whole, and although independent, they are also interdependent in that the one affects the other. Inasmuch as humans can become unhealthy from too much stress, so can a company. You cannot split mind and body in people. Neither can you split the 'mind and body' of a company. The aim should, therefore, be to achieve holistic company health which tends to optimal performance. The same argument applies to your home and family life or to any other cohesive unit that needs to function holistically, or where you have to interact closely with others, such as a sports team, etc.

30 It is not work that kills, but worry

Role ambiguity

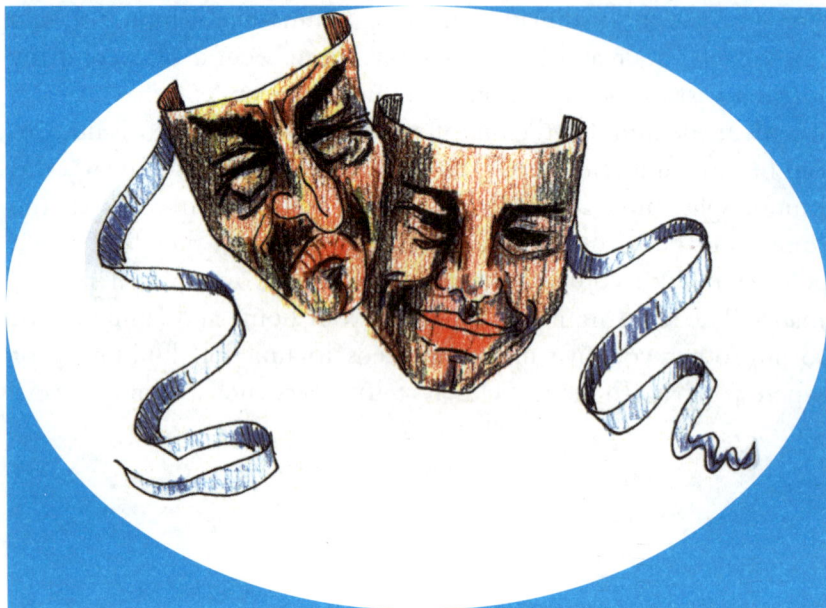

Inadequate or inappropriate role descriptions or job descriptions are often at the very basis of stress and frustrations. At work they can result from issues such as role ambiguity and conflict, and an over-lapping of boundaries that negatively affect your own image of your occupational profile and pride in what you do. You might be expect-ed to perform tasks that you don't enjoy, have no or little training for or that were not in your job description, and even if you want to, *will is no skill*, and *'tis skill, not strength that governs a ship*. Expertise in one field does not guarantee expertise in another, but can guarantee stress if you do not acquire the necessary additional skills to prevent it. People are frequently promoted to a management position because they are professionally or occupationally skilled in a particular field and not because of good management skills required for running large organisations. An outstanding worker on the production line becomes the foreman or supervisor; an outstanding scientist ends up as a professor with the responsibility of having to run a big academic department; an outstanding professor ends up as the vice chancellor and principal of a university; and so on. An even more stressful scenario can be created if people end up in management positions with no professional, occupational or management skills but because of some other decree. Role conflicts can also arise where role reversals occur. For example, a woman might work all day (her role as an employee), and then have to go home where she is expected to be mother, housekeeper and wife. Consider the increased stress caused by the additional time such a woman is required to spend on the hours she works at home, which is a form of 'unpaid overtime'.

31 More haste, less speed

Type A personality

The greater your need for haste, the more likely you are to put pressure on yourself. The Latin form of this proverb comes from the paradox *festina lente* ('Hasten slowly'), and an old African proverb states that *hurry bequeaths disappointment*. The need for haste can cause high stress levels which can be maintained by certain personality characteristics, such as found in the **type A personality**. Such a person is characterised by a sense of time urgency or 'hurry-sickness' and simultaneous involvement in multiple tasks (much of which centres around a need to be in control at all costs), a constant struggle to achieve, an impatience at anyone or anything that gets in the way, with irritability and aggressiveness at the forefront. Ego involvement is quite high in every task, resulting in an aggressive, defensive and possessive attitude contributing to misunderstandings, tension and more stress. These traits can be manifested elsewhere but are often demonstrated at work. This behaviour pattern is associated with con-

stant self-imposed demands which can affect your health negatively. The resultant aggressive component and chronic struggle to achieve more in less time with exaggerated hostile behaviour are particularly bad for stress and health problems. As opposed to this behaviour pattern, the **type B personality** manifests a less intense and slower moving, easy-going manner, is slower to be aroused by anger, and is generally more relaxed. The **type C personality**, on the other hand, comprises a behavioural pattern of excessive passivity, co-operativeness and emotional nonexpression. Ideally you should strive to modify the negative aspects of your behaviour pattern to improve and increase your level of achievements in a healthy and beneficial manner.

32 Time is money

Time management

Time is as valuable as money. Use it as such. Don't squander it. There are other proverbs on the theme of time management, such as *time flies* from the Latin *tempus fugit, one of these days is none of these days* and *procrastination is the thief of time*, meaning that if you continuously defer things you waste a lot of time and might end up doing nothing at all. *Tomorrow never comes*. In the saying *take time by the forelock*, time is represented as a bald person with only a lock of hair on the forehead. You can only catch time from the front by seizing the forelock which means taking advantage of your time **now**. Acquire

effective time-management skills. Manage your time, don't just spend it. *Time spent in vice or folly is doubly lost.* Don't make the mistake of thinking that time management only applies to your work situation. It is much more than that and affects your whole life. It's not so much that you plan to fail, but that you fail to plan. Better planning is an essential element of good time management, but plans and good intentions are useless unless you follow them through with positive action. *Fine words butter no parsnips* and *actions speak louder than words.* Time itself is not always the main stressor, but it is your perception and use of time. Don't feed on the misperception that there will always be enough time. *Time and tide wait for no person.* Neither tide nor time will tarry for you. Poor time management is often the result of poor self-management, giving rise to much stress. Better self-management leads to better time management which will result in increased productivity, less stress and best of all – more time for fun and relaxation. Don't forget also, that *time is a great healer.* However great your grief or disappointment, your pain will heal in time. Time has a wonderful healing quality, so set aside time for yourself to restore your body and mind's equilibrium.

33 Variety is the spice of life

Lifestyle

Stress can be related to your lifestyle. Without a break in your daily, weekly, monthly or yearly routine your life will become very monotonous and stressful. In the poem "The Task", William Cowper wrote:

> *Variety is the very spice of life,*
> *That gives it all its flavour.*

Make the necessary lifestyle changes. Set time aside to do something different as an antidote to daily pressures. Take regular breaks during working hours (stretch your legs, get some fresh air), go away for weekends, take regular holidays, etc. Unless you enjoy some recreation, you will become stressed and your health and productivity will suffer in consequence. Practise relaxation, make more of an occasion of meal times (avoid those TV dinners and programmes that interfere with communication and sometimes digestion), listen to music, get up earlier to start your day in a more relaxed way, find a non-competitive hobby, do something creative, stop and smell the flowers, enjoy nature. The natural sounds of birdsong, crashing waves and the smell of flowers are nature's own tranquillisers. Give yourself some time-out without feeling guilty, and balance your **right-brain activity** with your **left-brain activity**. Your left-brain activity involves the systematic, rational, logical part of your brain and controls movements on the right side of your body. Your right-brain activity involves the intuitive, creative, imaginative part of your brain, and controls the left side of the body. Don't live in a clutter. The appropriateness of this for stress management is reflected in the say-

ing that *there is a time and place for everything.* Life is much more pleasant if everything is in its proper place and you know where to find
it when you need it. Likewise your life will go much more smooth-
ly if your daily routine is not a cluttered one.

34 A healthy body, a healthy mind

Physical exercise

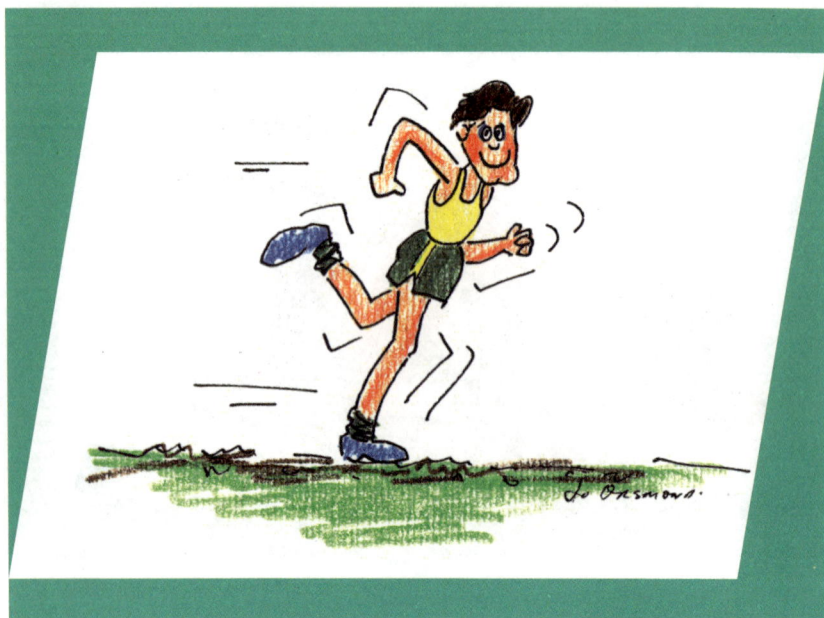

Exercise as a healthy pastime is encapsulated in another old saying, *there's nothing so good for the inside of a person as the outside of a horse*. This refers to horse riding, but in a broader sense, to other forms of exercise. If you are healthy and physically fit, you can cope better with stress. Even in ancient times this was recognised, as reflected by Juvenal's dictum, *mens sana in corpore sano* ('a sound mind in a sound body'). Regular physical exercise should be an ongoing endeavour, because as technology advances people become more inactive and use less energy. By incorporating regular, appropriate physical exercise into your lifestyle, you'll experience less routine anxiety, effectively reduce depression, improve your sleep patterns, and promote psychological wellbeing. Physical exercise also takes care of the arousal state caused by the fight-or-flight response, keeps your body in tone, reduces the risk of developing disease, strengthens your immune system, improves your cardiovascular health, helps control weight, increases your stamina, promotes breathing, and gives your lungs a work-out. It is important to choose an exercise regimen that you enjoy, because the enjoyment of it acts as motivation. The difference between motivating yourself (or someone else) and simply moving is whether the activity is enjoyed or not. If you enjoy it, rather than simply expecting some benefit, you are motivated, which provides that additional commitment and dedication to do your very best. If there is a benefit in it plus enjoyment, you are doubly motivated. Simply increasing the benefit by itself might move you and make you complain less, but it won't motivate you unless you enjoy the accompanying activity. The same applies to other tasks in your life, including your work.

35 Breathing bespeaks body and mind

Breathing correctly

Even if you don't physically exercise you should practise regular correct breathing exercises which promote relaxation, can help you regulate your heart rate, circulation and digestion, and assist you to control tension and stress. Your breathing can also help with healing, and is closely related to your state of mind and mood changes. It also is a means of communication and part of your body's nonverbal mode of expression, as well as a function of your speech. Although breathing is a fundamental prerequisite for life, it is one of the most easily

disturbed functions, and even minor mood changes or stress levels can affect your breathing, causing it to become shallow or strained or resulting in hyperventilation leading to lightheadedness or even fainting. You are familiar with the many forms of breathing that express your moods, such as sighing, breathlessness caused by emotion or fear, sobbing, screaming, laughing, and the experience of 'your breath being taken away'. Correct breathing should ideally be through the nose, predominantly abdominal (that is, diaphragmatic), and involve equal inspiration and expiration cycles (that is, it should have the correct rhythm). Most people naturally inhale first. Make yourself comfortable, focus on your breathing, and then concentrate on exhaling first. This allows the air to be taken in more efficiently, deepens respiration, helps to strengthen and condition your **pulmonary system** and your **cardiovascular system**, and promotes oxygenation. Recent research has shown that inhaling oxygen can improve mental agility and some authorities have referred to oxygen as one of the so- called 'smart' drugs of the future which could maximise brain activity, improve blood flow and enhance productivity.

36 Spare to speak and spare to speed

Assertiveness

The implication here is that if you are reluctant to speak out, you will not make much progress in life. *Better to ask the way than go astray.* Therefore, it is sometimes necessary to be assertive when communicating your requirements to others in order to reduce stress. Assertiveness describes a form of behaviour which enables you to communicate your needs, wants and feelings clearly, confidently, and truthfully towards others, without abusing their human rights in any way. Knowing the difference between assertiveness, aggressiveness and submissiveness is important. Aggressive persons tend to deny the rights of other people in favour of their own, and use demands or threats to achieve a win or lose result. This is a 'fight' response which can result in conflict. Submissive persons tend to deny their own rights in favour of those of others, being a 'flight' response to avoid conflict. By contrast, the assertive person negotiates a win–win solution, and does not demand rights at the expense of others. Although *truth seeks no corners* or *truth needs no colours*, assertiveness does not mean speaking up simply for the sake of saying something, for *every ass likes to hear itself bray*. Also, *a person that demands misses not, unless the demands be foolish*. If you feel that you need to be more assertive, ask yourself what you want and, if you believe it to be fair, ask for it as clearly as possible. *The language of truth is simple. Call a spade a spade.* Speak plainly and to the point, and say exactly what you mean, using uncomplicated language. You should be able to express positive and/or negative feelings, refuse requests without feeling guilty, and express personal opinions without causing further stress.

72

Do ✓

- Be calm and relaxed
- Express your feelings openly
- Give and take compliments easily
- Give and take fair criticism

Don't ✗

- Beat about the bush
- Go behind anyone's back or gossip
- Try to bully your way through
- Call people names
- Bottle up your feelings

A person that is angry is seldom at ease

Don't bottle up negative feelings

Research shows that just letting rip, can intensify anger and does not always get rid of it. Dealing with anger must be done **appropriately**. If you become violent or lose your temper, you then lose psy-

chological control, which is counterproductive for effective stress management. An Icelandic proverb states that *wrath often consumes what goodness husbands*. No matter how bad things are, you can always make the situation worse by losing your temper. This results in irrational behaviour and more stress. Endlessly rehearsing grievances and creating a hostile predisposition will just pump up your blood pressure further. Controlling yourself will make you feel better. *When a person grows angry, reason rides out*, and *when wrath speaks, wisdom veils its face*. Don't express your anger in the heat of the moment. Simmer down first by counting to twenty, and then, if necessary, express it **appropriately**. This will give you time to rethink the situation. Anger often depends on your perception that you have been insulted. This could be a complete misperception. Give the other person the benefit of the doubt. Be guided by what you hope to accomplish, don't just blow off steam. *Anger restrained is wisdom gained*, and *violence begets violence*. Similarly, don't be a victim of the saying *the tongue ever turns to the aching tooth*. That is, don't allow your thoughts to keep coming back to things that worry you. If you have problems with other feelings, deal with them and bring them out into the open **appropriately**. *Open confession is good for the soul*, and *a fault confessed is half redressed*. Ease the pain of your grief or unhappiness. The wisdom of these proverbs provides medicine that will heal your mind, more so than you realise.

38 Let bygones be bygones

Get rid of emotional baggage

Do your emotional house cleaning. Stop feeling as if you are a victim of the past and carrying the emotional baggage of it with you. *Forgive and forget. A mill cannot grind with water that is past,* which has two meanings. Firstly, the mill can be turned only by water currently passing, not by water that passed yesterday – that is, you cannot use time that is past. Secondly, there is no point in worrying about the past – you have to live in the present. Persistent intrusive thoughts about negative aspects of the past can cause stress, disrupt your sleep, and when they become part of your coping style, contribute to depression. Such **ruminative** coping will eventually develop into a thinking style that promotes self-defeating behaviour. Don't let it be the case for you that *the golden age was never the present age,* or *jam tomorrow and jam yesterday, but never jam today.* This last proverb comes from *Through the Looking Glass* by Lewis Carroll and implies that if there is one day that you enjoy more than the others in the week, today is never that day. The past is *water under the bridge.* You can't change it. You can do something about your **present** though. If you do not want to create future emotional baggage, don't hurt others' feelings. *Words cut more than swords,* and *A word spoken is past recalling,* as demonstrated in *The Rubáiyát* by Omar Khayyàm:

> *The Moving Finger writes; and, having writ,*
> *Moves on: nor all thy Piety nor Wit*
> *Shall lure it back to cancel half a Line,*
> *Nor all thy Tears wash out a Word of it.*

Dealing with these issues will help you to develop a more positive feeling of self-esteem, and will improve your self-image and self-confidence.

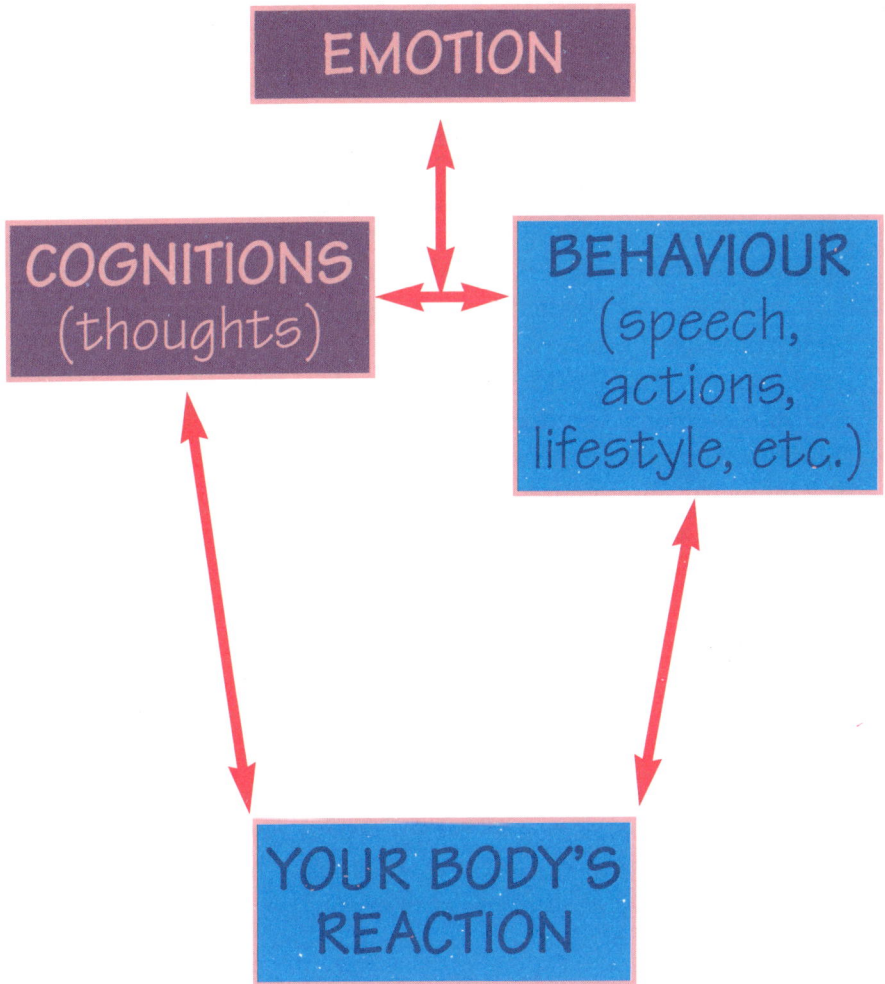

EMOTION

COGNITIONS (thoughts)

BEHAVIOUR (speech, actions, lifestyle, etc.)

YOUR BODY'S REACTION

39 When all people speak, no person hears

Cultivate people skills

The cultivation of good people skills is essential for good stress management. This is clearly illustrated in many parts of this book. Unless people listen to each other, they will learn nothing. However, the basic requirements for good interpersonal skills rest particularly on effective communication, which in turn includes appropriate body language, good speaking skills, good listening skills and effective conflict resolution and negotiating skills. Not only is communication essential for stress management, but in the modern technical world good communication skills are critically important for success. You can also overcome communication barriers and promote better communication by developing some of the basic characteristics of a pleasing personality, such as sincerity, honesty, flexibility, compassion and empathy as well as a positive attitude, and not being judgmental or inconsiderate. *A soft answer turneth away wrath.* This implies that you should not shout back when someone gets angry and shouts at you, because if you reply quietly and politely you are more likely to control the situation. *Pouring oil on the fire is not the way to quench it.* If you wish to pacify someone, don't say anything that will cause even more anger and push up the stress levels of both of you. Often perceived communication, rather than actual communication, is at the root of the problem, and breakdown in communication frequently contributes to loneliness, whether it occurs at home, socially or at work. So, *speak fitly, or be silent wisely.*

Appearances are deceptive

Be aware of body language

As you shouldn't judge people merely from outward appearances, so too you should watch your own and other people's body language. Other variants on this theme are: *All clouds bring not rain*, *still waters run deep*, and *truth has a good face but bad clothes*. Awareness of body language is an important part of stress management, and stress is readily reflected in nonverbal communication. *Things are not always what they seem* and *all are not merry that dance lightly*. Be aware of the signals that your body language and that of others communicate. People don't always express their emotions openly but sometimes indirectly through nonverbal behaviour such as body language. *Those that have to wait on you always have to carry the smile*, meaning that although they might seethe inside, they don't show their true feelings because you are the customer who is not supposed to be upset. Their body language, in fact, carries a different message which does not reflect how they feel. *They that are booted are not always ready. Fair face, foul heart*, and *fair without, false within* reflect the superficiality of outward appearance, and *bees that have honey in their mouths have stings in their tails* warns of the need for caution. Although body language is a common form of human communication, beware of judging by appearances – *never judge by appearances*,

for *none can guess the jewel by the casket*. An honest person may create the impression of being a villain. Therefore, *all are not thieves that dogs bark at*. On the other hand, *the cowl does not make the monk*. The person who wears a garment such as a cowl that covers the head may indeed be a villain disguised as a monk. But don't forget possible cultural differences in this regard.

41 There are always three sides to a story

Resolve conflicts

The three sides are: Your side, the other side, and the right side. This is something to consider when you practise conflict resolution and negotiation skills to reduce stress. You become frustrated when you encounter obstacles that block your goals. Frustration leads to conflict. This intensifies the stress. When your negotiating and coping skills fail to deal with the frustration associated with conflict, the resultant inadequate conflict resolution makes your stress worse. Frustration uses energy which can be better spent on resolving the conflict. Conflicts cannot be resolved angrily or hastily. *Anger and haste hinder good counsel. Hear all parties* and *give credit where credit is due* because *fair play's a jewel*. So seek less frustrating, conflict-resolving alternatives that can be readily implemented to decrease your stress levels. Negotiating and conflict resolution also require times when it is better to listen and be silent than to speak. Be aware, therefore, while *speech is silver, silence is golden*. The value of this is also taught by the proverbs *a person cannot speak well that cannot hold his tongue* and there is a time to speak and a time to be silent.

42 Give and take

Life is a two-way process

Aim for a **WIN-WIN** solution to achieve harmony and reduce stress. Don't assume a superior manner, for *a cat may look at a king*, and an old African proverb teaches that *the rain falls on every roof*. You should accept and make concessions and be as willing to help and forgive others in the same way as you want to be helped and forgiven. Do not negotiate others into a corner, but give them an honourable way out. That is, ensure that solutions to problems that cause stress are found that are mutually beneficial. This also requires a degree of foresight, because *a person is wise who looks ahead*, and *a word before is worth two behind*. You do not want to reduce your stress levels at the expense of increasing other peoples' stress levels. Your approach should be co-operative, not competitive or revengeful. The fact that anybody can make a mistake has been emphasised for centuries, as in the Latin saying *humanum est errare* ('to err is human') by Seneca. *The noblest vengeance is to forgive.* In *An Essay on Criticism*, Alexander Pope (1688-1744) wrote: *Good nature and good sense must ever join; to err is human; to forgive, divine.*

43 There are two sides to every question

Change stress-producing perceptions

Every medal has two sides, and so has every argument or stressor. If you want to reduce the effects of a stressor, look at the problem from another side. A necessary first step in the process of managing the effects of a stressor is to give up any stress-producing perceptions and to replace them with less damaging ones. The way in which you look at the particular stressor in your life will, to a large degree, determine whether the stressor will have a negative or positive effect on you. Stressors alone are not the only culprits. Some people in fact view life events or daily hassles as challenges rather than stressors. There are always different ways of looking at the same problem. Don't rigidly stick only to your one perception (or misperception) of the stressor, but reappraise it and look at it from other angles. This can also help you to change positively, because alternative perceptions can influence your interpretation and reaction to stress, which will modify your thinking patterns, and positively affect your emotions and feelings and ultimately your behaviour. Aim for that 'aha' experience, a feeling you get when you develop insight because your internal 'psychological light' has suddenly been turned on. Don't become bogged down in detail that clouds your perception of the overall situation. *Some people cannot see the wood for the trees.* Metaphorically speaking, you only see the trees because you become so involved in detail that you cannot see the issue as a whole. *Psychological insight* can be achieved by thinking about how others would see a similar situation and by constantly testing whether your stress-producing perceptions are true or not. Then seek alternative ones that produce less stress.

TEST YOUR PERCEPTION

True? False?

When the well is full, it will run over

Psychological self-empowerment

This saying has a similar meaning to *the last drop makes the cup run over*, or *the last straw breaks the camel's back*. The implication is that if something, although apparently small in itself, gets to you after many troublesome things, it eventually produces a feeling of being overwhelmed. You might put up with problems for as long as you can, but the resultant stress can ultimately give you such a sense of being overwhelmed that you feel that you are not psychologically in control. There are times when you might feel that *misfortunes never come singly* and you are so pressurised that you are losing the very control you need to perform optimally. Don't deal with this cautiously, for *untimeous spurring spills the steed*. ('Untimeous' means 'untimely' and

'spills' means 'spoils'.) The implications are that attempts to speed up the natural course of events could be more destructive than constructive for you. Rather take control and change yourself to achieve **psychological self-empowerment** to prevent that sense of being overwhelmed by stress and squeezed by life, for *a person that falls today may rise tomorrow.* Be guided by the proverbs *use makes mastery, where there's a will, there's a way, little by little and bit by bit,* and *little strokes fell great oaks.* Given enough practice, experience, patience, perseverence, time and determination, you will succeed.

45 Catch not at the shadow and lose the substance

Identify the real problem

Don't waste your time on trivialities and neglect the essentials. Problem solving to aid in stress management requires six basic steps. The first two are to: a) recognise that there is a problem; and b) identify the real one. Quite often the stressor that you are confronted with is not as clear cut as it first seems. For example, when you get home from work after a stressful day, you have an argument with your spouse. At first glance this appears to be simply another argument. However, on thinking it through, you remember the major traffic jam on the way home and your irritation. This adds a new dimension to the problem. Yet another aspect is revealed later when

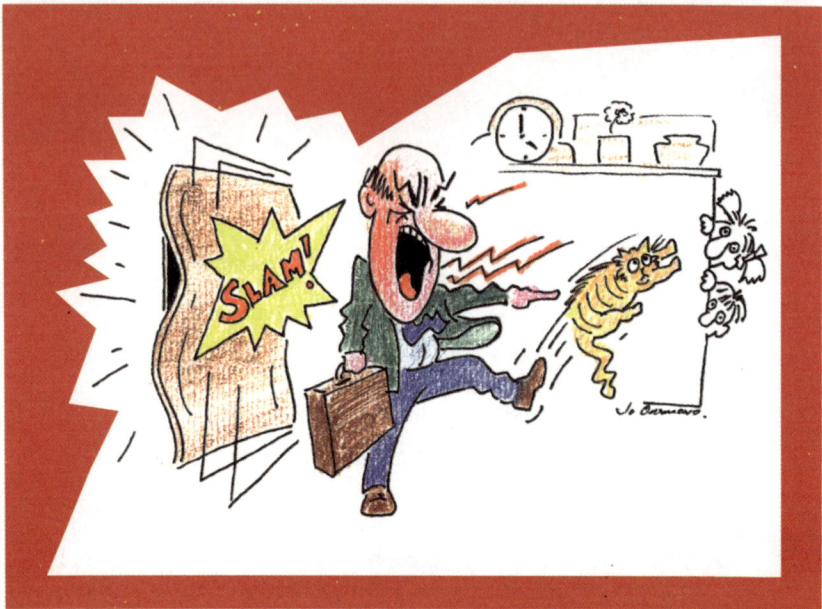

you discuss work-related pressures with a friend. So, is there a problem? If so, what is the real problem? Is it the argument with your spouse, the traffic stress, or the work stress? Are you using a defence mechanism to distort reality, and displacing the real issue onto a different one? Establish clearly what the problem is. But don't forget that *there is no royal road to learning* – a proverb based on a reply given by Euclid (300 BC) to Ptolemy I, when he wanted to know whether there was an easy way to master geometry. To know the answer also requires a certain degree of education, experience and wisdom. Don't be scared to admit a mistake, for *experience is the mother of wisdom*. That is, out of experience you'll get wisdom as you learn by your mistakes. *Trouble brings experience and experience brings wisdom*, for *it is a great point of wisdom to find out one's folly*. Once you've completed steps a) and b), move on to the next four steps: c) devise a strategy; d) execute it; e) evaluate your progress towards your goal; and f) consider potential barriers you might encounter. These are explained in the next two sections.

46 All things are difficult before they are easy

Learn problem-solving skills

When you initially attempted to walk, ride a bicycle, drive a car or any other seemingly difficult task you weren't sure how you would succeed, but as you continued to practise, and took it step by step, it became so easy that you wondered why it was difficult in the first place. Knowledge cannot be acquired all at once. You gain it step by step. *Learn to walk before you run.* You cannot spell 'categorical', if you haven't learnt to spell 'cat'. In a similar way, you can learn to acquire problem-solving skills when you are faced with a problem that causes you stress. Having recognised and identified the true problem, divide it into small units which you can manage individually. This will help with the sense of being overwhelmed. Tackle each of these units individually by applying heuristics (rule-of-thumb guides gleaned from your experience, intuition, background and training). Now assess whether the problem-solving skills you have applied have led to the desired outcome. If so, then carry on, if not, return to the beginning and start the process again. Should you exhaust your efforts, seek help from other appropriate sources, and explore potential barriers to your problem-solving skills. Once you have resolved the first phase of the problem, determine how acceptable your solution is to others involved. By following the sequence I have outlined, you will learn to develop a problem-solving, rather than a problem-creating mode of thinking. By practising these problem-solving skills, you can attain the mental skills and efficiency to master stress caused by problems. *Practice makes perfect.* You do not achieve this just by talking about it or watching others, and *if at first you don't succeed, try, try, try again*, for *ninety per cent of inspiration is perspiration.*

A TECHNIQUE FOR PROBLEM SOLVING

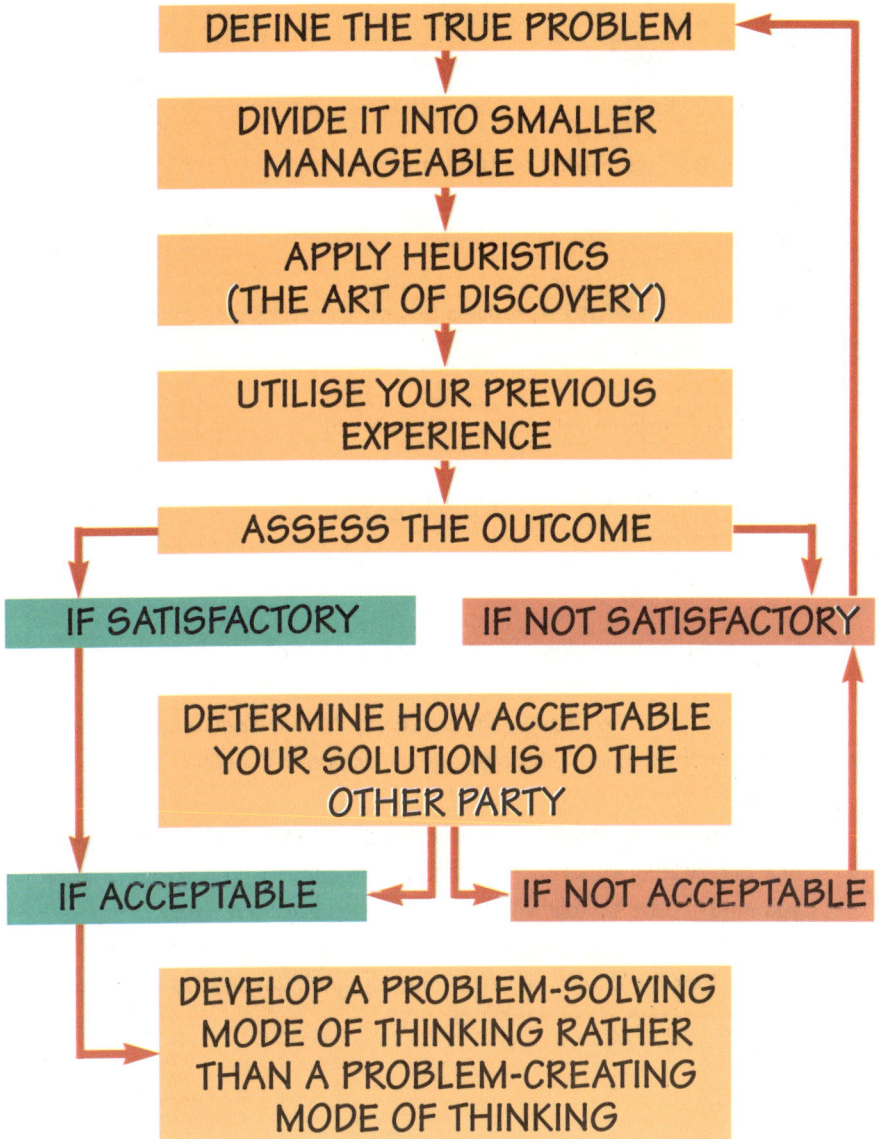

DEFINE THE TRUE PROBLEM

DIVIDE IT INTO SMALLER MANAGEABLE UNITS

APPLY HEURISTICS (THE ART OF DISCOVERY)

UTILISE YOUR PREVIOUS EXPERIENCE

ASSESS THE OUTCOME

IF SATISFACTORY

IF NOT SATISFACTORY

DETERMINE HOW ACCEPTABLE YOUR SOLUTION IS TO THE OTHER PARTY

IF ACCEPTABLE

IF NOT ACCEPTABLE

DEVELOP A PROBLEM-SOLVING MODE OF THINKING RATHER THAN A PROBLEM-CREATING MODE OF THINKING

Necessity is the mother of invention

Explore barriers to problem solving

Sometimes you are forced to find another way.

Are you:

✳ Reluctant to repeat or practise any of the steps described for problem solving?

✳ Biased towards investigating alternatives?

✳ Reluctant to entertain opposing points of view?

Do you:

✳ Have enough knowledge of the relevant problem?

✳ Use functional fixedness (the tendency to consider only the usual function of an object and overlook other possible uses).

✳ Use methods guaranteed to solve problems even if you don't understand how they work (such as algorithms consisting of a set of rules you simply have to follow like a recipe when baking a cake).

✳ Always look for 'cookbook' solutions? Life just doesn't work that way.

✳ Know how to access information? A vast storehouse of knowledge and information is available, and the trick is to know how to access it. This is also a key difference between using your intelligence for problem solving and the artificial intelligence of a computer.

✳ Use creativity (flexible, imaginative thought processes that go beyond your present knowledge and recognise that problems can be solved in more ways than one). Creative people tend to be nonconformist, independent, confident, curious and persistent. They know that fortune favours the bold. They use more divergent thinking (exploring novel ideas and side paths) and less convergent thinking (aimed at finding a single correct answer).

✳ Stick to one mental set (the tendency to attempt to solve new problems with the same old procedures). This may become habitual. People do more things through habit than through reason. These habits may sometimes be helpful, but they are unhelpful when you require fresh insights. They make you cling to old ways and blind you to new breakthroughs, for habits are at first cobwebs, at last cables.

48 The weakest link is the weakest think

Correct your thinking errors

The strength of the chain is in the weakest link. If only one link is weak, no greater strain can be placed on the chain than that single weak link can take. The same applies to your thinking. One weak 'think' or 'thinking error' can affect your entire stress response. So, identify and change your thinking errors (cognitive distortions). *A person that believes all, misses; a person that believes nothing, misses.* If your thinking interferes with your ability to resolve stress, remember that *thinking is very far from knowing*, and *the wish is father to the thought*, meaning that you believe what you want to believe – whether it is an error or not. The way you think also has to do with self-fulfilling prophecy or labelling theory. There is plenty of psychological evidence to show how this can affect every part of your life. For example, patients' responses to treatment can be significantly affected by their thoughts and beliefs about whether they are going to recover or not. The more positive your thinking, the better your chances. People also perform according to the expectations they and others have of them. If you persistently label yourself or someone else a failure, chances are you or that person will start believing what you think and live up to it. So, be positive and make your thinking work for you, not against you. *Let not your wits go woolgathering.* If you want to reduce stress, you obviously have to start by changing the processes within the brain which produce the stress in the first place. Your aim should be to develop stress-reducing as opposed to stress-creating thinking, for *there is nothing either good or bad but thinking makes it so* (From Shakespeare's *Hamlet*).

EXAMINE THESE COMMON THINKING ERRORS AND IDENTIFY AND CHANGE THOSE THAT APPLY TO YOU

* Are you an all-or-nothing thinker? Do you think in extremes or absolutes? If you do, you are setting up your thought patterns to discredit yourself endlessly.

* Do you overgeneralise, expecting uniformly bad results because of a few bad experiences?

* Do you use a mental filter, screening out positives and only concentrating on negatives?

* Are you an automatic discounter, discounting the good things in your life which will reinforce your poor self-esteem and feelings of being a second-rate person?

* Do you jump to conclusions before you have all the facts?

* Do you magnify or minimise the problem?

* Do you use emotional reasoning or do you reason with the facts?

* Do you use 'should' statements, and live in the past or the future, thereby permitting today to pass you by?

* Do you apply negative labels to yourself or others? If so, you or they might live up to those labels.

* Do you personalise issues by taking everything personally?

Look on the bright side

Optimism

Be optimistic. An optimistic and positive outlook will help you cope better with stress and can even affect your health positively. Optimists have a challenging rather than a passive approach to life. They would argue never say die. They never give up, but press on and tend to regard stress as external in that they do not always feel that they could have caused the situation, and believe that things will improve. For them *every cloud has a silver lining*, which means that the sun is still shining, even if they can't see it. Their perception is that *when one door shuts, another opens,* **when things are at**

the worst they begin to mend, *the darkest hour is that before dawn,* and *after a storm comes a calm.* These proverbs optimistically suggest that inevitably there must be something better after unpleasantness and highlight the differences between pessimists and optimists. Pessimists tend to perceive stress as internal and blame themselves. There is a link between pessimism and not coping with stress. *A person of gladness never falls into madness.* For the pessimist *it is misery enough to have once been happy.* Pessimism also tends to produce more unhappiness and psychological problems which in turn negatively affect the immune system and, therefore, health. *The wound that bleeds inwardly is most dangerous.* Optimism favourably tends to affect achievements, rates of depression, health, coping skills, and interpersonal relationships. Pessimists tend to be lonelier, because *when good cheer is lacking, our friends will be packing.* The concept of 'learned optimism' has recently been developed whereby pessimists can be helped to think more optimistically. This research has shown that pessimism is a characteristic that is eminently changeable by changing your perceptions and thinking. So, start smiling at the world.

50 Laugh and the world laughs with you, weep and you weep alone

Humour

What applies to optimism also applies to humour when it comes to stress management. If you are in a cheerful mood, it is easier to get on with people than if you are solemn, which tends to make people keep away from you. Although the concept behind the above proverb dates from long ago, it was given its current form in 1883 by Ella Wheela Wilcox in her poem "Solitude":

> Laugh and the world laughs with you,
>   Weep and you weep alone,
> For the sad old earth must borrow its mirth,
>   But has trouble enough of its own.

Laughter is the best medicine, and *mirth is the sugar of life.* When you laugh there is simultaneous contraction of some fifteen of your facial muscles and irrepressible exhalations of your breath. You might sometimes also use laughter in other ways to relieve stress, such as when you are unsure of yourself or nervous. However, laughter at the expense of someone else can also contribute to stress. Laugh with someone, not at someone. An appropriate sense of humour contributes to healthy stress, and reduces unhealthy stress. It has a positive effect on the arousal state arising from the 'fight-or-flight' response, and helps to improve interpersonal communication, can assist in conflict resolution, can resolve emotional tension, and can place a different perspective on problems that cause stress.

Don't dig your grave with your teeth

Watch your diet

Inadequate dietary habits contribute to stress. At the same time stress can contribute to the depletion of essential nutrients in the body. Further, dietary sources of essential nutrients such as vitamins and minerals can prove inadequate during periods of disease. An inappropriate diet can contribute to certain diseases, whereas a correct diet can contribute to their prevention. Modern research shows that what you eat or do not eat may,

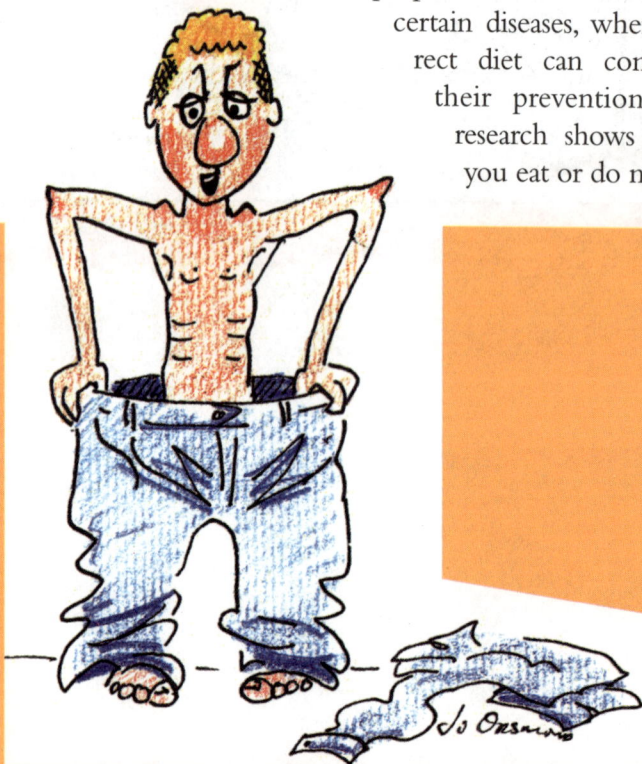

therefore, very well determine how you die. This is reflected in old proverbs like *kitchen physic is the best physic, an apple a day keeps the doctor away, the mouth is the executioner and the doctor of the body* (a good diet may kill or cure), *feed by measure and defy the physician*, and *eat to live and live to eat*.

The cause-and-effect relationship between stress and nutrition can lower your adaptability to cope with stress. Most people can protect themselves from normal stress by living a healthy lifestyle which includes a nutritious well-balanced diet. This also means not overindulging. When *the eye is bigger than the belly* you overestimate the capacity of your stomach. *The best doctors are Dr Diet, Dr Quiet and Dr Merryman*, the implication being that a sensible diet and a quiet and cheerful spirit are the surest remedies for ill-health. Don't skip meals and then make up for it with an onslaught of food later. Apart from the disadvantages of depleting your body and mind of a steady supply of nutrients, sudden large amounts of food in a short time sends your body's coping mechanism into overdrive with resultant feelings of drowsiness. Authorities recommend at least five servings of vegetables and/or fruit a day, an increased intake of fibre and unrefined grain products, and reduced fat consumption.

52 The beginning of health is sleep

Get enough sleep

Early to bed and early to rise comes from Benjamin Franklin's precept:

> *Early to bed and early to rise,*
> *Makes a man healthy, wealthy, and wise.*

Stress is closely associated with sleep disturbances, which can also be complicated by a number of medications and other substances such as alcohol and drinks or food that contain stimulants like caffeine. At the same time too little or irregular sleep can contribute to elevated stress levels and an increased inability to cope with stress. *One hour's*

sleep before midnight is worth two after. You should get enough sleep because your brain and your body need sleep to deal with stress. The function of sleep is primarily restorative and is crucial for normal thermoregulation, conservation of energy and stress management. *Sleep is better than medicine.* Sleep disturbances can be a symptom of various psychological and medical disorders, and of stress, as well as being stressful in themselves. Furthermore, they can significantly diminish your resistance to cope with such disorders and with the resultant stress. The right amount of sleep is also important. This should not be an excuse for overindulgence, for *a person who sleeps all morning, may go begging all the day after,* and *nature requires five, custom takes seven, idleness takes nine, and wickedness eleven.*

53 Well is, that well does

Improve your wellbeing

Wellbeing includes the themes of hope, courage, faith, the support of others, a love of life, making the necessary lifestyle changes, and exploring your own personality. *A person gets a double victory who conquers the self.* Mental health is not freedom from stress but an overall balanced lifestyle. Use visualisation and imagine your mind as an

empty television screen, or as the philosopher Locke put it, a *tabula rasa* ('blank slate'). You can select what you want to put on it or which channel you want to focus on. Choose the wellbeing programme. Even simple visualisations of place or experience can have immediate positive effects on your wellbeing. Let your mind work for you, not against you. Don't be inflexible and resistant to change. *Change brings life.* Change harmful attitudes and beliefs, and deal with specific negative emotions, such as guilt, fear, anger and resentment. *Living well is the best revenge* and *pardons and pleasantness are great revenges of slanders.* Learn to forgive, for *a person who forgives others, God forgives.* Develop the ability to recover quickly – bounce back. An African proverb says, *the African race is an India rubber ball; the harder you dash it to the ground, the higher it will rise.* Transform failure into success and put meaning into your life. *Nothing succeeds like success* and *a person seems wise with whom all things thrive.* Put yourself in charge psychologically, so that you don't feel a victim of circumstances. Develop your own personal mission statement. Visualise yourself sometime into the future. Where would you like to be? *Hope well and have well.* Now try and live according to that mission statement to promote healthy stress and make you a **WINNER**! *Win gold and wear gold.*

Know thyself

Analyse your stress

To cope effectively with stress, it is important for you to get a clear picture of the problems you have with stress. You can use the following two simple techniques to assess your own stress levels and responses: a **stress checklist** and a **stress monitoring record** which you can also use as a daily wellbeing diary. It helps you to tap into your stress responses, so that you can understand them and teach yourself more appropriate responses by changing your perceptions and thoughts about the stress. As you've seen, your response to stress can be divided into physical, psychological and behavioural reactions. To make this clearer, divide your assessment of your stress into these reactions. They also relate to your social interactions because that is where you often express your stress response: *a person that is ill to the self will be good to nobody.*

STRESS CHECKLIST OF THE GENERAL SYMPTOMS OF UNHEALTHY STRESS

Make a ✔ if you experience the symptom often (at least once a week or more) and an ✗ if you experience it sometimes (less than weekly, but at least monthly). If you score three or more for any one of the categories, then you are beginning to show stress in that particular category and should take appropriate action. Look again at the stress curve to see where you fit. Do you experience:

PHYSICAL REACTIONS

UNUSUAL TIREDNESS	X	HIGH BLOOD PRESSURE		ERRATIC BOWEL FUNCTION	X
APATHY/LACK OF ENTHUSIASM	X	SEXUAL PROBLEMS		FREQUENT INDIGESTION	
BREATHLESSNESS FOR NO REASON		UNEXPLAINED HEAD-ACHES/PAIN		UNEXPLAINED NAUSEA	
FEELINGS THAT YOUR APPEARANCE HAS ALTERED FOR THE WORSE	X	FEELING FAINT OR UNUSUALLY WEAK FOR NO REASON	X	FEELING TIGHT-CHESTED FOR NO REASON	
DIFFICULTY IN RELAXING		MUSCLE TENSION		DIZZY SPELLS FOR NO REASON	
DISTURBING DREAMS/ NIGHTMARES		FEELING PHYSICALLY UNWELL		EXCESSIVE PERSPIRA-TION FOR NO REASON	

PSYCHOLOGICAL REACTIONS

FEELINGS OF HELPLESSNESS		FEELINGS OF DISLIKING YOURSELF	✓	FEELING THAT YOU CAN'T COPE	✗
FEELINGS OF DEPRESSION		BEING AFRAID OF DISEASE		FEELINGS THAT YOU ARE A FAILURE	✗
FEELINGS THAT NO ONE UNDERSTANDS YOU		AN INCREASE IN COMPLAINTS ABOUT WHAT HAPPENS TO YOU		FEELINGS THAT OTHER PEOPLE DISLIKE YOU	✗
FEELINGS OF GENERAL ANXIOUSNESS		LOW SELF-ESTEEM/ LOW OPINION OF YOURSELF	✗	FEELINGS OF CONFUSION	✗
PHOBIAS (IRRATIONAL FEARS)		FEELINGS OF BEING GOSSIPED ABOUT	✗	FEELINGS OF CONCERN, MAINLY FOR YOURSELF	
AWKWARD FEELINGS WHEN CLOSE TO OTHERS	✗	BEING OVERLY SELF-CRITICAL		FEELINGS OF FREQUENT CRITICISM	
FEELINGS THAT YOU HAVE FAILED IN YOUR ROLE AS A PARENT, SPOUSE, CHILD, EMPLOYEE, EMPLOYER	✗	FEELINGS THAT NO ONE WANTS TO WORK WITH YOU	✗	FEELINGS THAT YOU HAVE BEEN NEGLECTED OR LET DOWN	
PANICKY FEELINGS		FEELING TENSE AND KEYED UP		FEELINGS OF LONELINESS AND NO ONE TO TALK TO	✗
BEING UPSET BY DISEASE IN OTHERS		PERSISTENT GUILT		A LACK OF SELF-CONFIDENCE	✗

BEHAVIOURAL REACTIONS

MEMORY LOSS/ FORGETFULNESS	X	DIFFICULTY IN MAKING UP YOUR MIND		DISINTEREST IN OTHER PEOPLE	
POOR LONG-TERM PLANNING	X	DIFFICULTY IN SHOWING/ EXPRESSING YOUR TRUE FEELINGS	X	SUPPRESSED OR UNEXPRESSED ANGER	
POOR CONCENTRATION	X	WORRYING		FEARFULNESS	X
INCONSISTENCY		SOCIAL WITHDRAWAL	X	POOR DECISION-MAKING	X
INABIBLITY TO MEET DEADLINES	X	MAKING UNNECESSARY MISTAKES		UNCO-OPERATIVE RELATIONSHIPS	
POOR TIME MANAGEMENT	X	THE NEED TO WORK LATE REGULARLY		FEELING DISGRUNTLED/ MOODY/IRRITABLE	X
PROCRASTINATION	X	POOR WORK QUALITY	X	EMOTIONAL OUTBURSTS	
THE NEED TO TAKE WORK HOME CONSTANTLY		DIFFICULTY IN COMPLETING ONE TASK BEFORE RUSHING ON TO THE NEXT		GREATER USE OF ALCOHOL, CAFFEINE, NICOTINE, MEDICINES TO COPE	X
POOR PROBLEM-SOLVING SKILLS		THE NEED TO CANCEL LEAVE		FIDGETING/ RESTLESSNESS	X
ACCIDENT-PRONENESS		NAIL-BITING		UNPREDICTABILITY	
LOW INTEREST IN WORK		AN EXCESSIVE APPETITE	X	A LOSS OF APPETITE	
A DROP IN PERSONAL STANDARDS	X	ENGAGING IN FREQUENT CRITICISM OF OTHERS		THE NEED TO CRY FOR NO REASON	
INCREASED AGGRESSIVENESS		FRANTIC BURSTS OF ENERGY		TICS/NERVOUS HABITS	
LACK OF INTEREST IN LIFE	X	LITTLE SENSE OF HUMOUR		SLEEP DISTURBANCES	

STRESS-MONITORING RECORD

This is an example of what your stress-monitoring record could look like. It means keeping a stress record by writing down your responses when they occur or as soon as possible afterwards. The information you gain from doing this exercise will help you to learn more about your own unique reactions to stress, so that you can change them and learn to cope better with stress. Change them by changing your perceptions and thinking. Practise this technique whenever you feel the need to change your stress response from a negative to a positive one.

ANTECEDENTS	STRESS REACTIONS	CONSEQUENCES
I was getting up to make a speech/ presentation	1. PHYSICAL Shortness of breath/trembling	A dry mouth/tension
	2. PSYCHOLOGICAL Anxious/feeling that I would make a fool of myself	Couldn't find the right words
	3. BEHAVIOURAL Apprehension/worrying/ poor concentration	Poor communication

55 Action is the proper fruit of knowledge

It all starts with you

Everything must have a beginning. Even impressive undertakings start small. Take that initial step to turn your negative stress into positive stress. You have remarkable powers of self-healing. Don't leave them untapped. **You** have to **believe** in **yourself**. *A good beginning makes a good ending.* When you do endeavour to manage your stress, remember the four E's, for *a tree is known by its fruit*. Start to take charge of **your life today**.

IF IT'S TO BE, IT'S UP TO ME.

4 E's

E fficiently

E ffectively

E conomically

E legantly

REFERENCES

Fergusson, R. *The Penguin Dictionary of Proverbs*. London: Penguin Books, 1983.

Kaplan, H.I. and Sadock, B.J. (Eds.) *Comprehensive Textbook of psychiatry/VI*. Sixth Edition,Vols. 1 and 2. Baltimore, Maryland: Williams and Wilkins, 1995.

Rice, P.L. *Stress and Health*. Second Edition. Pacific Grove, California: Brooks/Cole, 1992.

Ridout, R. and Witting, C. *The Macmillan Dictionary of English Proverbs Explained*. London: Macmillan, 1995.

Schlebusch, L. *Conduct Disorders in Youth*. Durban: Butterworths, 1979.

Schlebusch, L. (Ed.) *Clinical Health Pscychology. A Behavioural Medicine Perspective*. Halfway House: Southern Book Publishers, 1990.

Schlebusch, L. (Ed.) *South Africa Beyond Transition: Psychological Wellbeing*. Pretoria: Psychological Society of South Africa, 1998.

Sternberg, R.J. *In Search of the Human Mind*. Orlando, Florida: Harcourt Brace, 1995.

Wilson, F.P. *The Oxford Dictionary of English Proverbs*.Third Edition, Oxford: Oxford University Press, 1990.